Quiltmaking

ABOUT THE AUTHOR

Ann-Sargent Wooster is a sculptress and painter as well as a quilter. She is also the author of THE ART REFERENCE GUIDE. Miss Wooster has attended the Silvermine College of Art, the Parsons School of Design, and the School of Visual Arts. She is currently working for her doctorate in Art History at Hunter College of the City University of New York. She is particularly interested in contemporary art and plans to become an art critic.

Quiltmaking

The Modern Approach to a Traditional Craft

by Ann-Sargent Wooster

GALAHAD BOOKS · NEW YORK CITY

© Ann-Sargent Wooster, 1972
Library of Congress Catalog Card Number: 74-15433
ISBN 0-88365-154-8
Manufactured in the United States of America
Published by arrangement with Drake Publishers Inc.

This book is dedicated to my Mother
whose unfinished quilt got me started.

Table of Contents

Introduction

This book explores how to make and design traditional and modern quilts using classic and current methods. But what exactly is a "quilt?" The simplest definition is any textile sandwich of three layers stitched together to cause them to function as one layer. The three layers of a quilt are called: the "top" (upper most layer), the "fill" or "filling" (the middle layer), and the "backing" (the bottom layer). "Quilting" is the process of joining the three layers together. Each chapter of the book explores a facet of quiltmaking.

The first chapter is a dictionary of standard quilt types and terms. If you open the book randomly it is an excellent source of information about a term that is found for the first time out of its original context.

Chapter two and chapter three discuss making and designing patchwork and applique, the two standard ways of making a quilt top. "Patchwork" is the seaming of pieces of cloth together to create patterns. The patterns are usually geometric. The act of sewing the units or pieces of cloth together is called "piecing." The other name for a patchwork top is a "pieced" top. A completed pattern is called a "block" and most patchwork quilts are made from six to twenty-five blocks joined (set) together. Chapter two presents the structure of patchwork designs and stresses the growth of patterns from simple geometric units or systems.

"Applique" is more lavish than patchwork. It lays a smaller piece of cloth onto a large one and holds it in place with hemming or machine stitches. This type of top is alternately called an applied top. The term applied top also refers to tops made with embroidery, batik, and paint. The third chapter details the methods of sewing applique, transferring old patterns, and how to go about designing new ones.

The fourth chapter deals with the final stage of making a quilt, that is, quilting it by joining the three layers together either with handsewn running stitches or on the sewing machine. The fourth chapter also describes how to build a quilting frame, how to put the quilt in the frame, how to ply your needle in this new setting, and how to avoid using a frame by using a sewing machine instead.

Patchwork, applique, and quilting may be applied to making objects other than bedcovers. The ways in which these techniques may be adapted to creating clothes and decorative objects are discussed in chapter five.

Recently, many painters, sculptors, and designers have been turning to soft materials to create their designs. Chapter six is a gallery of a new quilts and new forms with the comments of the artists on what made them choose this media and what methods they used to construct their works.

Dip into the book at any point. Begin with the modern forms and work back to traditional styles or copy several traditional patterns and then begin creating your own designs; start by making quilts and then begin collecting them or start as a collector, thrilled by the beauty of design and craftsmanship of old quilts, and then commence turning your hand at making your own quilts. Whatever approach you choose, create, explore, and enjoy.

A QUILTING DICTIONARY

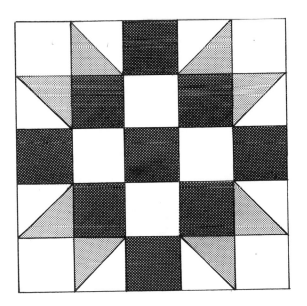

Allover Design—A pattern which covers the quilt top from edge to edge with regular small units and which does not have a border.

All White Quilt—A plain top usually made of white material but which was also made with colored silks on which elaborate quilting was the sole decoration. The design was emphasized and given higher relief by the insertion of extra padding through small slits made in the back after the design was quilted. This style reached its highest development abroad in the sixteenth and seventeenth centuries, however, examples can be found of "all white quilts" dating from the eleventh century. Pieces in America were made by the higher social class, and most quilts in this style date from the late eighteenth and early nineteenth centuries. The invention of the Jacquard loom in 1804 was the probable reason for the decline in padded quilting. It was possible to obtain similar effects with less effort using the Jacquard machine, and there developed the so-called Marseilles spread which had a long period of popularity.

Album or Presentation Quilt—A quilt made up of elaborate blocks each created and stitched by a different woman. Sometimes a general motif was agreed upon, but usually design and materials were the choice of the individual woman. The blocks were set together and presented as a token of esteem in a public ceremony to a respected person such as a minister or community leader. The blocks were often signed with india ink or embroidery by the women who made them.

Applique—From the French word, *appliquer* meaning to put or lay on. The name describes any form of applied top in which fabric, in pure design or representational images, is hemmed onto either a plain square or a piece of cloth the size of a bed.

Autograph Quilt—A quilt used to collect and display the signatures of friends or famous people. Friends were asked to donate a block with their names inscribed in India ink or embroidery, or famous people were sent patches of the quilt and asked to autograph them. The quiltmaker incorporated the signed patches in her design.

The Back—The bottom layer of a quilt. It is made from a sheet, a blanket, or print or solid yard goods which were seamed together.

Binding—Finishing the raw edges of an otherwise completed quilt. This is done in several ways: a narrow edge of backing can be turned over on the top and hemmed down; the edges of the back and top can be turned in and run together; a separate strip of cloth, picking up one of the colors of the quilt top or in a contrasting color, is stitched around the quilt. Commercial hem facing or twill tape is now also used. They can be turned back over the edge and hemmed. This is the best method because binding wears out and must be periodically renewed.

Blind Hemming—see Hemming.

Block—One complete pattern. It may be any size from very small to big enough to cover a bed. A top is usually made from a number of appliqued or pieced squares or blocks set together flush or interspersed with plain blocks or lattice bands.

Border—A band which surrounds the quilt proper and serves as a frame. It may be made of plain, pieced or appliqued material. In the past, plain borders allowed space for the quilter to display her art.

Comforter—A very thick quilt of from three to four inches in depth. (A normal quilt is only one quarter to one half an inch in thickness.) In recent years the handmade comforter has been replaced by factory-made nylon or satin-covered dacron ones stitched together in large open figures. Comforter is another name for a tied quilt in the West.

Coverlet—The coverlet which covered only the bed (not being made large enough to cover the pillows) was the most popular sized quilt. It was used primarily for warmth.

Crazy Quilt—First a product of Colonial necessity and later a Victorian fad, it is a quilt top made on either foundation blocks or on a piece of cloth the size of a whole bed. The quilt top is made of scraps in various sizes or colors fit together like a puzzle.

Feathering—A method of decoration in which a shape is outlined with small "Saw Tooth," half square triangles. It was a common way of ornamenting plain shapes.

The Fill or Filling—Sheet cotton, dacron, or wool called batting which is placed between the top and the back of the quilt. In times of scarcity, an old blanket, an old quilt, newspapers, or corn husks were substituted for materials especially designed for filling a quilt.

Foundation Block—A piece of soft cloth such as muslin which was cut to the desired size of a block or an entire bed and which was used as the underlying structure for building the "pressed quilts," "Crazy" quilts, and appliques.

Friendship Quilt—A quilt expressing American neighborliness. Each neighbor gave a block, and all met to sew the quilt together. The quilts were for people going West, to help a family get on its feet after a fire, to celebrate a marriage, or to honor a minister, teacher, or hero. The blocks were generally decorated with applique, but embroidery or piecing were also used.

Hemming—The process by which an edge is turned under and sewn down with small stitches. Regular hemming is made with small slanting stitches on the right side. Blind hemming is done like hemming but with larger stitches through the fold and with only one thread on the right side. Hemming is used to attach applied pieces of fabric in appliqued designs or to attach the binding after it has been turned under.

Lattice Strips—Strips of plain cloth from two to four inches in width is used to outline and join pieced blocks. To avoid a rigid grid which would dominate the pattern, squares the width of the strip but of a different color are set where lattice strips intersect each other.

Marking—The process by which preparatory to quilting, the quilt design is drawn on the quilt. Sometimes this is done freehand, but normally a perforated pattern; tin, wood, or paper shapes; or household implements such as string, glasses, or spoons are employed in tracing the quilt pattern in pencil or blue chalk on the top.

Marriage Quilt—A variety of friendship quilt. Around 1700 an engaged girl invited her friends to her home to see her wedding presents and help her quilt her Wedding Quilt, the last of her thirteen requisite quilts and the only one that could contain hearts and other symbols of love. Because the superstition grew up that it was bad luck for the engaged girl to work on her own Marriage Quilt, it came to be the custom that the friends of the bride (and in one unusual case the past girl friends of the groom) each brought a block to the engaged girl's house, set them together, quilted the top, and presented the quilt to the girl as a wedding present. The custom spread throughout the country as people moved West. Around 1900, this custom died out.

Masterpiece Quilt—A quilt which displayed the epitome of the quiltmaker's designing, sewing, and quilting ability. In the East, the careful piecing of diamonds in "The Lone Star" and "The Star of Bethlehem" was considered the height of skill and gave prestige to their makers. In the Middle and Far West, appliqued quilts were considered more difficult, and women made the "Horn of Plenty" or the allover "Garden Wreath" to display their expertise as needlewomen. Masterpiece Quilts were worked on when the quilter was rested and the light was good. A work or utility quilt was usually begun at the same time and was worked on whenever the conditions were less favorable. The term is still in use today.

Medallion Quilt—A quilt made by choosing a central motif (such as a scarf commemorating a place or an event, a picture chintz, or an embroidered or appliqued design) and building out from it in concentric framing strips which may be fancy pieced work, applique work, or plain cloth. The quilt either told a story or was pure design. This quilt type was popular from 1700 to 1830 but can still occasionally be found today at country fairs.

Padding—A process by which portions of a quilt design are raised. Stems and thin scrolls are made by inserting thick string under the top while it is being quilted. Broad areas are thrust into relief by inserting extra batting after the pattern is quilted. This is accomplished by making a small hole in the back of the quilt and using a knitting needle or other pointed implement to push wadding through the hole until the design is stuffed full.

Patch—(noun) Two or more pieces of fabric sewn together to make a pattern. A synonym for block. Also, used to mean a single unit of a pattern.

To Patch—(verb) Precisely, to hem a small piece of cloth down on a larger one, in other words to applique. However, it is used interchangeably with piecing. It is a misunderstood and misused word.

Patchwork Quilt—Strictly, a pieced quilt, but it is generally used to refer to all types of quilts.

Piece—(noun) A small section of cloth that goes to make up a block.

To Piece—(verb) To join pieces of cloth together with a seam to make a block.

Pieced Quilt—A quilt made of small patches or units sewn into blocks. Seventy-five per cent of American quilts, Dolores Hinson says, were made of scraps of cloth cut into geometric shapes and sewn (pieced) together to make a quilt top.

Pressed Quilt—A way of joining patches. A piece is first sewn on a foundation block with a running stitch. The second piece and all subsequent pieces are placed face down, right sides together on the preceeding piece. A seam is made through both patches and the foundation block. The piece is then "pressed" open and is ready for another piece to be added. "Log Cabin," "Pineapple," and "Grandmother's Fan" are all examples of "pressed" quilts.

Puff—A comforter. Colloquially a tied quilt in New England.

Putting In—The act of fastening the edges of the back and top of the quilt to the quilting frame with the fill spread evenly between. When one neighbor would say to another, "I put in yesterday," it meant that she had put a quilt in the frame.

Quilt—Any bed covering with a stitched

interlining.

To Quilt—(verb) The act of joining three layers of material together. It may be done by hand with small running stitches or on the sewing machine.

Quilt Top—The uppermost layer of material of a quilt. It may be pieced, appliqued, embroidered or decorated in any manner.

Quilting Frame—A usually home-made stretcher made from four strips of wood ordinarily one inch thick, two to four inches wide, and ten to twelve feet in length. The four corners of the frame are fastened together with wooden pegs thrust through holes that had been pierced through the ends of the four strips of wood. A series of holes is necessary to allow the width of the frame to be adjusted. The frame corners are today more commonly fastened with metal "C" clamps purchased in any hardware store. Along the edges of the frame, an inch width of heavy cloth is firmly tacked. The quilt was pinned or basted to the cloth and stretched taut between the frames. Historically, the frame was supported on four quilting chairs which are now known by antique dealers as "arrowbacks," "Windsors," "fan-backs," "Hitchcocks," and "low ladder backs." Today such a frame would be balanced on saw horses or, as one young woman in Brooklyn, New York is currently doing, suspended by ropes from the ceiling with pulleys.

Fixed and tilt-top quilting frames are available from needlework shops and large mail order companies such as Sears Roebuck. Although quilting may be done without a frame in your lap or on the sewing machine, the frame has the advantage of holding the quilt in position and maintaining a uniform tension.

Reverse Applique—A method of applique in which two or more layers of cloth are sewn together. The top layers are cut through revealing the underneath layers. The cut edges are turned under and hemmed. South and Central American *molas* are made in this technique.

Rolling—A quilt in a frame is first quilted along the edges. When that is done, the completed portion is wound up by turning the end frames over and over so that the unquilted section may be reached. "I'm on my third roll" meant that enough quilting had been done so that the quilt had to be rolled three times to get to the reachable space. Ruth Finley explains, "As five or six rollings completed the work, unless the quilt was very large, to name the 'roll' one was working on was a definite way of stating how nearly the quilt was finished."

Running Stitch—A simple stitch used for quilting, basting, and piecing in which the needle goes in and out of the cloth usually picking up two or more stitches at a time.

Scrap Quilt—A quilt made from dressmaking or other scraps. A scrap quilt top utilized a great variety of fabrics, each block often being pieced from a different combination of materials. It was therefore not necessary to have a large quantity of one material on hand to piece these tops. Scrap quilts are often more beautiful than quilts with regular, homogeneous designs because the need for "making do" forced on the quiltmaker a kind of irregularity that leant itself to the production of striking and unique quilts.

The Set—The material for and the

method of setting the blocks together. "I've begun my set" meant that the unfinished blocks were being joined to form the whole.

Setting Together—Sewing the finished blocks together. This is done by either simply sewing the blocks flush, or more commonly, by separating the worked blocks with plain blocks or strips of cloth in one or more colors.

Taking Out—Removing the quilt from the frame. In the past people said, "She took out this week," meaning that the woman in question had completed quilting her quilt and had taken it out of the frame preparatory to binding it.

Template—A pattern made of paper, cardboard, or cloth for patchwork pieces or a pattern made of paper, wood, or tin for quilting designs. These may be drafted by the quiltmaker, or in some cases, they may be commercially purchased.

Throw—A coverlet just large enough to cover the top of the bed. It got its name because it was the right size to be thrown over a person who was napping. Victorian "Crazy" quilts are the most common quilt form worked in this size and purpose.

Tied Quilt—The simplest form of quilting in which the top is merely joined to the fill and the bottom by means of yarn or thread pulled through at regular intervals and then knotted. The tufts of yarn were frequently left as decoration. Tying is used when time is at a premium, or when no fill is used so that elaborate quilting is not warranted, or when the top is too thick to permit easy passage of the quilting needle.

Trapunto or Italian Quilting—These terms refer to a way of making high-relief designs favored by Kentucky mountain women. Through two or more layers, the design is outlined with a double row of running stitches. Rug yarn or orlon bulky yarn is drawn through the double lines of quilting throwing the design into strong relief.

PATCHWORK

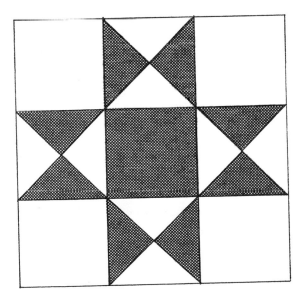

"Patchwork" or "pieced work" is a method of making a quilt top by seaming together small pieces or units of cloth. These pieces are usually geometric shapes cut from scraps. When sewn together, they make a single pattern called a "block." A block may be any size from very small to the dimensions of a bed. The blocks are sewn together flush or separated with strips of cloth or plain blocks. The act of arranging the blocks and joining them is known as "setting the quilt together."

The following basic steps will give an understanding of how patchwork is made.

7

1. First decide what type of quilt you want.

A "bedspread" is used primarily in the daytime and should cover the bed, the mattress, and the pillows.

A "coverlet" is used for warmth at night. It does not cover the pillows but should, if necessary, be ample enough to cover a large or heavy person.

A "throw" is usually four by six feet and is used to cover a sleeping person.

A "crib quilt" or baby quilt covers a child sleeping in a crib. It is either two by three feet or three by five feet.

When making a bedspread, use a tape measure and measure the length of the mattress from head to foot, the width of the mattress from side to side, and the depth of the bed from the top of the mattress to the floor or the dust ruffle. This will give you the size of the quilt. The following standard bed sizes may serve as a guide for your estimates: (Remember to add at least eighteen or twenty-two inches for the skirt of the quilt.)

Twin	39 × 75"
Double	54 × 75"
King	72 × 84"
Cot	30 × 75"

2. Collect a large box or bag of cloth scraps, either from your own sewing or from friends or a local dressmaker. If you want to make a quilt in an allover color scheme, you can purchase the material for the project.

3. Pick a pattern. The easiest way to select a pattern is to thumb through the patchwork section of this book and pick several you like. Decide on what size is appropriate to your purposes. The bigger the block, the more quickly it is pieced, however, keep in mind that some designs do not look right when made large.

4. Draft the pattern. The patterns given in this book have been grouped and developed according to their basic geometric units. Preceeding each section, a sample unit of the design is shown. This is of a size that may be easily sewn on the sewing machine. The sample unit may be traced and cut out or, following the instructions given, you may take a sheet of paper and fold a unit of any size.

The "template" (pattern of the unit) is given greater longevity by tracing it onto a piece of cardboard or a piece of heavy paper such as blotting paper. A durable template is necessary when many patches of the same shape must be cut.

Repeated cutting wears down the edges of the template thus altering its shape. This can throw the whole pattern out of line. Taping the edges with scotch tape is a way of preserving the contours. If the template becomes worn through repeated pinings, the paper may be restored by taping it.

5. Place the pattern on the cloth and pin. The patches should all follow the grain line. This lessens the possibility of puckering and warps which would have to be eased during the quilting.

6. Place two patches side by side and sew them together with a quarter of an inch seam with hand sewn running stitches or on the sewing machine.

In the past, papers the size of the finished patch were cut and inserted on the wrong side of the patch while sewing the patches together to insure the regularity of the seams. The papers were then taken out when the top was finished.

All seams should be pressed toward the center. Continue stitching the units together until the pattern (block) is finished. The back of a block will be a network of small seams (see plate 1). Make enough blocks to cover the bed. Less blocks may be made if they are going to be stretched by adding plain blocks between the pieced ones.

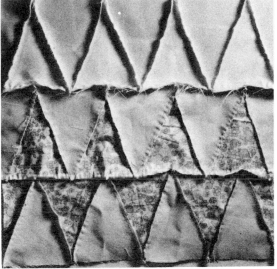

Plate 1

Practice drafting the patterns, cutting out the units, and sewing them together either by machine or by hand. This will enable you, even before you attempt a whole top, to develop a feeling for color and pattern as well as sewing techniques. The practice blocks need not be wasted. They can be turned into pillows (see chapter five).

7. Set the quilt together. You may join the blocks with lattice strips making a grid (fig. 2-1), or the strips may be interrupted with a square where four strips meet (fig. 2-2). Four large blocks may be set together in the center and surrounded with a wide border (fig. 2-3). Blocks also may be set side by side, flush or they might, as was very common, be separated with plain blocks (fig. 2-4) depending on

the pattern. The plain blocks were reserved for fancy quilting.

Square blocks can be set as diamonds. In a North Carolina "Saw Toothed Star" quilt (plate 2), pieced blocks were joined with plain blocks also set as diamonds. Another method of joining squares set as diamonds was by using zigzag strips. The blocks are set in this way in a North Carolinian "Cactus Basket" quilt (plate 19).

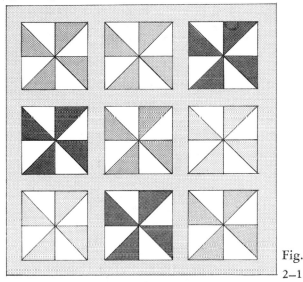

Fig. 2—1

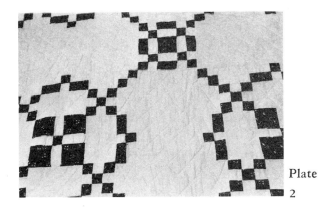

Plate 2

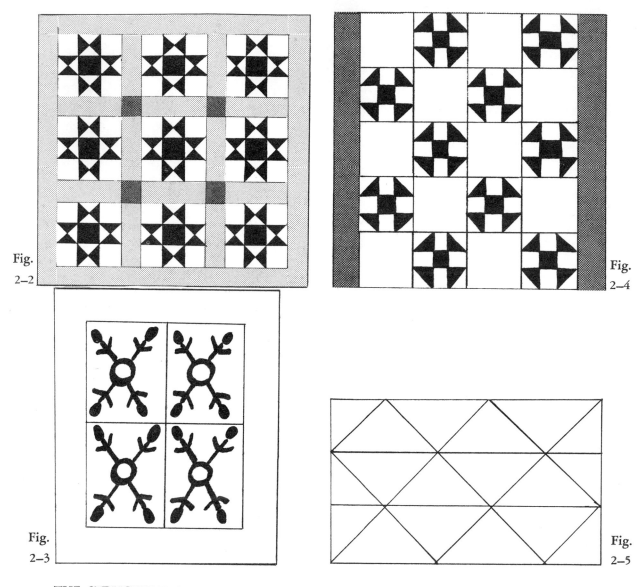

Fig.
2–2

Fig.
2–4

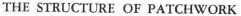

Fig.
2–3

Fig.
2–5

THE STRUCTURE OF PATCHWORK

Patchwork quilts are grouped according to how many units make up a block. The most common are one patch, two patch, three patch, five patch and nine patch blocks. To understand a design, you have to know how many patches it is made up of.

A *one-patch* quilt (fig. 2-5) is usually an allover design made from a single unit. A design built up from only squares such as "Hit and Miss" or triangles such as "A Thousand Pyramids" or hexagons such as "Grandmother's Flower Garden" constitute one variety of one patch quilts. The embroidered silk, satin, and velvet "Crazy" quilts of the 1880's through 1910

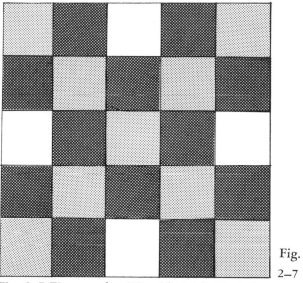

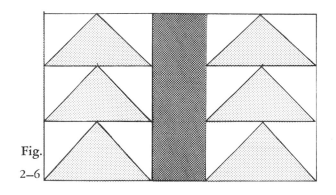

Fig.
2–6

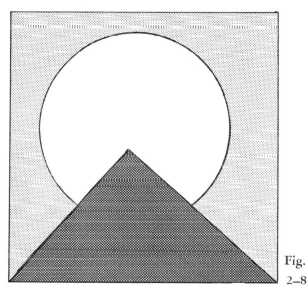

Fig.
2–7

Fig. 2–7 Five-patch—"Double Irish Chain"

Fig.
2–8

are another kind. A third type of quilt in this category is the medallion quilt. Medallion quilts were popular from 1700 to 1830 and were constructed by building out in borders from a central motif or square. A contemporary medallion quilt is found on page 76. Unless allover patches are grouped before the final piecing is begun, a quilt made by this method becomes more than a lapful before it is half-finished.

There are two main types of *two-patch* quilts (fig. 2-6): one type is pieced in lengthwise strips such as "Flying Geese"; in the second type the patch is cut in half, one half pieced in a pattern and the other half is plain or appliqued. The many basket quilts are of this second type.

Three-, *five-*, and *seven-patch* quilts (fig. 2-7) are fairly rare. The most popular of these is the single, double, or triple

"Irish Chain." It is a five patch, and, unlike other patch quilts, this means that there are twenty-five rather than five squares going to make up a block. The same is true of the seven patch. Each block is seven by seven squares, in other words, forty-nine squares in all. An example of a three-patch pattern is "Moon Over the Mountain" (fig. 2-8).

11

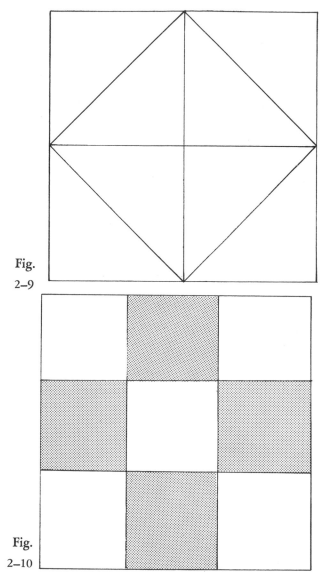

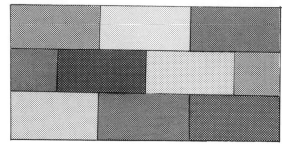

Fig.
2–11

Fig.
2–9

Fig.
2–10

Perhaps, the most popular of the quilt patterns is the *nine-patch* (fig. 2-10). The nine divisions are made by folding a square the size of the block into three equal parts twice—first side to side then top to bottom. The smaller squares can be subdivided into more intricate patches, but for a first quilt or a work quilt, many quiltmakers used the basic squares to make a design such as the "Double Nine Patch" (fig. 2-25).

A good way to develop a feeling for how patterns are composed is to make single blocks of patterns that appeal to you. Traditionally, when a quiltmaker saw a new pattern she liked, she went home and pieced a block of it then kept it in a drawer for future reference. Especially choice collections of these sample blocks were mentioned in wills and were left to a favorite daughter or granddaughter. If you are loath to them in a drawer, they may be made into pillows or a sampler quilt in which each block is a different pattern.

*   *   *

If a pattern can be divided into four equal parts, it is known as a *four-patch* (fig. 2-9). It is one of the most common bases for quilt patterns. The basic four units may be redivided as long as they repeat the divisions exactly from corner to corner. The four divisions are made by folding a square the size of the block in half twice—first side to side and then top to bottom.

Almost from the invention of weaving, a variety of quilting has existed. People reasoned that if one layer of cloth kept them warm, then three layers would keep them even warmer. The Chinese had always used quilted cotton to make winter garments. The Arabs learned quilting from the Chinese. When the crusaders were "rescuing" the Holy Land, they discovered that the Arabic quilted shirts would more effectively prevent their chain mail armor from chafing them than the single layer shirts they had been wearing. They brought the technique of quilting back with them, and it was readily adopted by their womenfolk. Both for necessity and beauty, in manor or cottage, the women stitched quilts.

The first quilting patterns were simple, but as the women developed greater proficiency with their needles in this area of handiwork, the designs proliferated and became more intricate. Distinctive family patterns were designed and passed down as heirlooms through the generations. In Northumberland and Durham, quilting became an important craft, and in that area there is a continuing quilting tradition that is still alive today through the work of the Rural Industries Bureau.

European quilts were made as part of a complete bedset which included quilts, bed curtains, canopies, and what is now called dust ruffles. These were made of the finest and longest lasting materials that could be afforded and were handsomely embroidered or appliqued and then quilted. They were meant to last for at least a lifetime and were most often cherished and preserved. The patchwork quilt did not appear in England before the eighteenth century by which time it had become the standard way of making quilt tops in America.

The earliest quilts in America were crude things, purely the result of necessity. The Pilgrims had brought quilts and blankets from their European homes, but when they wore out, there was not any cotton or wool cloth to make new ones. They therefore patched or "clouted" the cloths and bedclothes they had. A 1630 poem, "The Forefather's Song," describes this condition well.

And now our garments begin to grow thin,
And wool is much wanted to card and spin.
If we can get a garment to cover without.
Our mother in-garments are clout upon
  clout.
Our cloths we brought with us are apt to
  be torn,
They need to be clouted soon after they're
  worn,
But clouting our garments they hinder us
  nothing,
Clouts double are warmer than single whole
  clothing.

At first the women did not make quilts because the need for new clothing was even greater than the need for bedcovers.

An England greedy for revenue at first outlawed the manufacture of all cloth in the colonies. By 1640 though people were being encouraged to learn the arts of linen cloth manufacture. Each family was required by law to have the services of a full-time spinner. These were either children or unmarried women, hence the name spinster. "New England's First Fruits" written in 1642 enumerates the cloth available:

13

With cotton woll which we have at reasonable rates from the islands and our linnen yarne, we can make dimities and fustians for our summer cloathing; and have a matter of 1,000 sheepe which prosper well, do begin withal, in a competent time we hope to have woolen cloath there made.

Woolen cloth, linsey-woolsey (linen-woolen), homespun (cotton) colored with indigo and natural dyes were the only fabrics available to the Americans, and they took a long time to manufacture. Figured "calicoe" and "chints" had to be imported from England until well into the nineteenth century. All the small scraps left after dressmaking were prized and preserved and stitched together to make a new piece of cloth, a quilt top. Until the Industrial Revolution, there was never enough cloth to make the European style of quilt.

The earliest and simplest quilts were merely scraps, trimmed and stitched into a Crazy-patch quilt. Irresistably, women began to arrange the scraps into patterns and designs. The simplest form of organization was to cut all the scraps into uniform squares or rectangles. These were sewn together until the desired size was achieved. This was generally quite wide (eight to ten feet) because beds before the nineteenth century slept three or more people, and the quilt had to cover the extra wide bed, several mattresses and a trundle bed.

Strips were sometimes pieced horizontally. Bands of rectangles were placed so that the seams matched up on alternating rows. This type of ordering was called "The Brick Wall" (fig. 2-11) after the form of building construction it resembles.

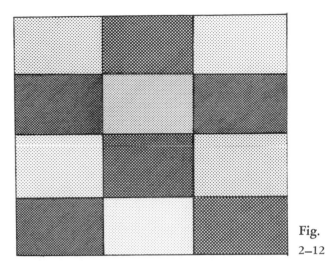

Fig. 2–12

In order to have an allover design incorporating many colors and producing a pleasing visual effect, the quiltmaker had to be able to keep the entire quilt in her mind. Early on, systems were developed which more easily insured a successful design. At first stripes were organized in two ways. One involved a simple alternation of light and dark rectangles in a vertical strip. This was known as "Hit and Miss" or "Hairpin Catcher" (fig. 2-12) when sewn so as to produce a checkerboard effect. In another type of strip or, as it was commonly called, "stripey" quilt, a vertical strip of dark patches was alternated with a strip of light patches. This was referred to as "The Roman Stripe" (fig. 2-13) and was considered extremely choice when the stripes were very narrow. If the quiltmaker had a great variety of fabric scraps available, the strips were graded light, medium, and dark.

The "Coarse Woven Patch" (fig. 2-14) is a variation of of these one-patch quilts based on the rectangle. Diagonal chev-

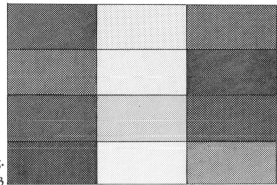

Fig.
2–13

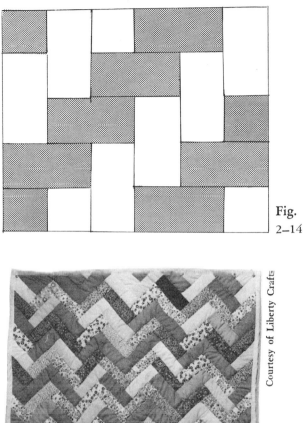

Fig.
2–14

rons are made from abutted rectangles. When the strips of chevrons are sewn together, an allover zig-zag effect is achieved. The quilt was made either as a scrap quilt with the rectangles being of many different colors or it was sewn so that strongly contrasting lights and darks would reveal the structure of the pattern. A modern cot quilt made by the Freedom Quilting Bee, Alberta, Georgia in the "Coarse Woven Patch" pattern (plate 3) is made from sunny reds, pinks, yellows, oranges, blues, and greens, all of the same value (lightness and darkness). This quilt makes color rather than structure the primary interest of the top.

When cloth became more available, instead of being pieced, "stripey" quilts were made from uncut, single-colored strips of cloth. In an 1860 Pennsylvania quilt, the quiltmaker has stitched together three bands of rainbow stripes—pink, red, orange, yellow, brown, blue, and grey which were separated and bordered with sprigged tan cotton. Quite appropriately the quiltmaker called her design

Courtesy of Liberty Crafts

Plate
3

"Rainbow Stripes" (fig. 2-15). The quilt is now in the Holstein collection, New York City.

15

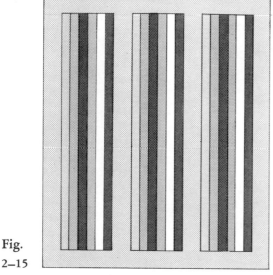

Fig.
2–15

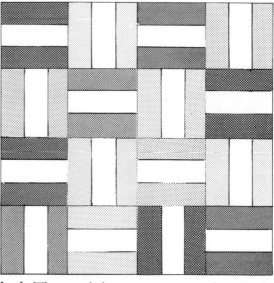

Fig.
2–16

In England stripe quilts were very common and were frequently used as an excuse for elaborate quilting which ignored the patches. One such example of this practice is a late nineteenth century quilt made in fawn and red, equal-width sateen strips by H. Evans of Carmarthenshire. It is quilted in banded medallions in an allover spiral pattern known in the Evans family as "snail creep."

A good place to begin the translation of traditional quilts into modern terms would be with a stripe quilt. The abstract stripe paintings of the contemporary artists Barnett Newman, Morris Louis, or Kenneth Noland might provide a starting point for a quilt design, or one can simply turn to nature to find the color and rhythm of the stripes. With colored pencils, crayons, or paint, it helps to draw a plan before buying the material. Approximately two and a quarter yards of each of four colors plus an additional two and a quarter yards of a fifth color for the border are needed to make a multi-colored striped quilt for a standard sized bed. The straight one quarter of an inch seams are quickly stitched on the sewing machine, and the whole top could be pieced in an afternoon.

"Stripey" quilts, like all one-patch quilts, tended to be quite bulky, and the quiltmakers began breaking the strips into blocks. One of the most basic blocks is formed by grouping the stripes into a three-patch block. A bright, cheerful 1873 New Jersey quilt has a three-patch block made by sandwiching white between two bands of the same color thus producing "The Roman Square." The blocks were placed so that the bands are alternately horizontal then vertical (fig. 2-16). In another variation of "The Roman Square" (fig. 2-17), each block is made up of three different colored narrow oblongs. The blocks were separated from each other by solid colored bars. When the fancy "Crazy Quilts" were the fashion, "The Roman Square" was made out of silks and velvets and banded in black.

In a nine-patch, two color variation of

16

Plate
4

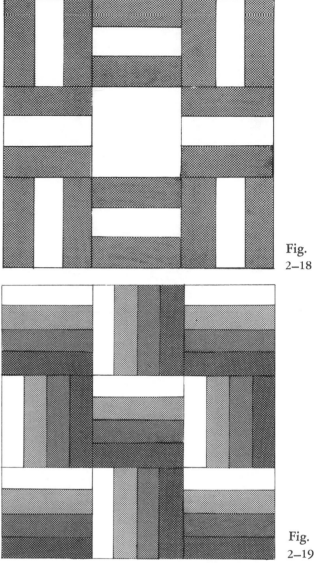

Fig.
2–17

Fig.
2–18

Fig.
2–19

Courtesy of Chocolate Soup

Plate
5

"The Roman Square" called "Beggar's Blocks" by most Americans but "Cats and Mice" by the Pennsylvania Dutch (fig. 2-18), eight small squares composed of two dark bands sandwiching a white center band are pieced around a central white square so that the stripes are alternately horizontal then vertical. In an entire quilt top made from this pattern, the pieced blocks would be separated by equal-sized white blocks.

A four-layered square was another popular way of quickly piecing small strips of cloth. Rachael Liberman used this block to make two very different crib quilts. One is the traditional "Jacob's Ladder" design (plate 4) in which four layers are arranged so that the layers line up to form stepped diagonals (fig. 2-19). The layers were prints colored blue and white, green, orange and purple, and light blue. The second quilt top features her own design which she calls "Centered Heart" (plate 5). In it the blocks are set so the dark half of the block faces toward and frames the central appliqued red heart.

SQUARES

Most patchwork designs are based on the square. Either small squares are employed to build an overall design or geometric shapes are fitted within a square block. It is important to use accurately measured and shaped squares.

The best way to fold a square (fig. 2-20) is to take a sheet of paper approximately the desired size with at least one true straight edge. A sheet of newspaper or a piece of writing paper would be fine. Take the upper left hand corner and fold it toward you until the left hand side lines up with the bottom edge. Cut along the right side of the triangle. Open the paper and you have a perfect square. If all the edges are not straight, it may be necessary to trim the piece.

There are some one-patch quilts such

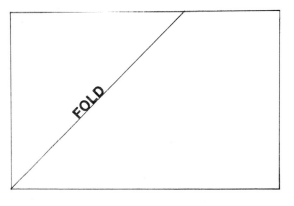

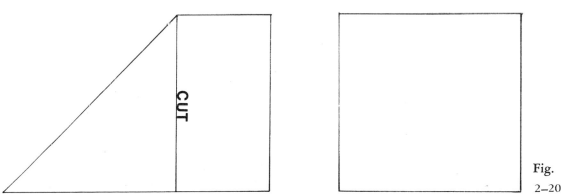

Fig. 2–20

Fig. 2–20 How to fold a square

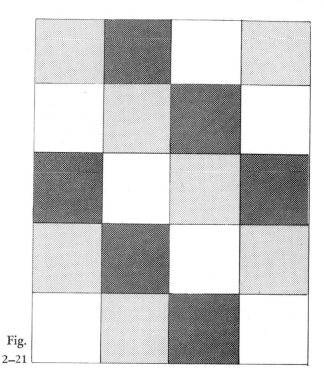

Fig.
2–21

Plate
6

as "Grandmother's Postage Stamp" (fig. 2-21) which are based exclusively on squares. To make this design, three or more colors are alternated in rows. In the first vertical row, colors *A, B, C are sewn repeating from the asterisk until the desired length is reached. In the second row, the colors *B, C, A are sewn, and in the third row, the colors are sewn in the order *C, A, B. In a three color quilt, the fourth column would repeat the first, the fifth column would repeat the second, and the sixth row would repeat the third. When this process is repeated across the width of the quilt, a stepped ladder effect is achieved. The tiny pink, green, and white squares in the unquilted "Grandmother's Postage Stamp" top which was used to make the jacket in plate 70 really are the size of a postage stamp and had

to be sewn by hand. The tie in plate 67 uses the same pattern but on a larger scale. The two and a half inch blue velveteen and blue and purple calico squares were easily pieced on the sewing machine.

One-patch quilts can be designed by simply piecing squares randomly in an allover design. The ordering is only subject to what pleases the eye of the quiltmaker. Precut boxes of squares are sometimes sold for making a quilt or skirt of this type, but serious quilters prefer the satisfaction of selecting their own fabrics and colors. Sometimes darker squares are grouped around a light center, or lighter squares are grouped around a dark center. Contemporary quilts in this design (which are especially popular in England and France) strongly resemble Paul Klee's "magic square" paintings.

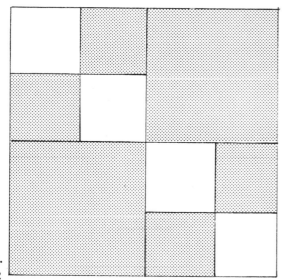

Fig.
2–22

Plate
7

In her baby quilts, Rachel Liberman of Cambridge, Massachusetts builds squares into stepped diamonds by layering them outward from a central square. The space between the dominating diamond and the outer rectangular border is filled with pieced strips of cloth the width of the central square and the length of the distance between the arms of the diamond and the outer rectangle. In one of her baby quilts, the diamond is of light colors set in a darker print (plate 6), and in another the diamond is three medium tones surrounded by pale-colored material (plate 7). For fabric she uses bright cotton print remnants from Woolworth's and Grant's. The quilting is done on the sewing machine and follows the large areas.

If it takes four squares to complete a block it is called a four-patch (fig. 2-22). A "Double Four-Patch" block (fig. 2-23) was made by folding a square into quarters then cutting along the folds. One of the quarter squares was folded into four smaller squares. One of the smallest squares was used as a pattern to cut out

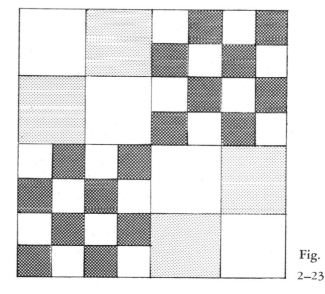

Fig.
2–23

21

Fig. 2–26 "Puss in the Corner" (block)

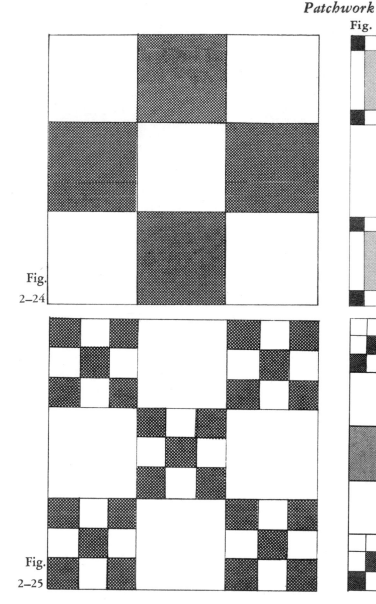

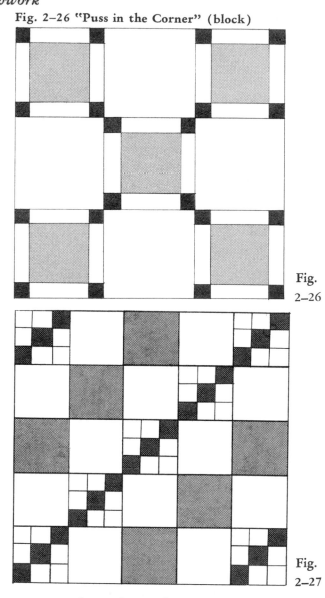

Fig.
2–24

Fig.
2–26

Fig.
2–25

Fig.
2–27

four squares of dark colored cloth and four squares of light colored cloth. Alternating light and dark, the little squares were pieced into two small four-patch squares. Another of the original quarter squares was folded into four twice thus making eight little squares. Using one of these smallest squares as a pattern, eight little squares of one color and eight little squares of another color were cut out. These were pieced together making two four by four checkerboards. The four squares were pieced together alternating the four-patch square with the sixteen-patch one.

When a square block is folded into thirds both lengthwise and crosswise, the result is nine small squares. When it takes nine such squares to complete a block, it

22

1 Embroidered Quilt, silk and cotton, made by Helen Bitar

2 Detail of Embroidered Quilt showing central embroidered medallion, made by Helen Bitar

3 Flowers of Dusk, solid colored cottons and silks, 4′ x 8′, made by Sophia Adler

4 Detail of Flowers of Dusk

5 Left side of Woman Clothed with the Sun, 1971-72,
applique and assorted fabrics, 6′ high, made by
Nell Booker Sonneman

6 Detail of Woman Clothed with the Sun, partial text on
the hem: "...and a moon under her feet and a crown of
twelve stars on her head," made by
Nell Booker Sonneman

5

6

is called a "nine-patch" (fig. 2-24). A nine-patch was one of the first quilts a young girl was set to do.

The "Double Nine-Patch" (fig. 2-25) is a pattern for a single block but also represents how the blocks of a nine-patch are set together. In the single block, five two-color checkerboards are joined by four light colored squares. A whole quilt top could be made from an alternation of pieced nine-square checkerboards set with plain blocks of the same size.

A late nineteenth century silk quilt from New Jersey (plate 8) shows how this simple unit, through an excellent choice and placement of fabric, can be transformed into as visually exciting a quilt as one with elaborate piecing. The nine-patch blocks are set as diamonds and are separated and bordered with a medium brown colored silk. Both of these patterns can be quickly made on the sewing machine.

The most common ordering of squares is to take two or more colors and ladder them diagonally across the surface of the top. This is called a chain. "Grandmother's Postage Stamp" is an allover chain, but many chains were worked as single blocks. One of the simplest of these is a "Nine-Patch Chain" (fig. 2-27) from the second quarter of the nineteenth century found now in the Shelburne Museum, Vermont. The three-color pattern is made from a pieced block and two plain ones. A basic sized square was decided upon. In two colors (colors A and B), two-thirds of the blocks needed to make the top were cut out in this size. The pattern used to cut the aforementioned squares was then folded and cut into nine little squares. For each block of

Plate 8

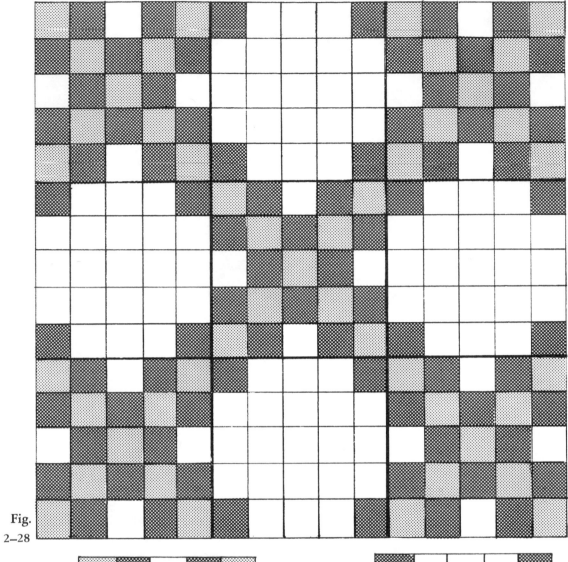

Fig.
2–28

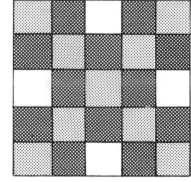

A

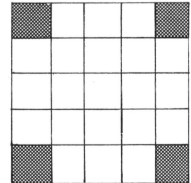

B

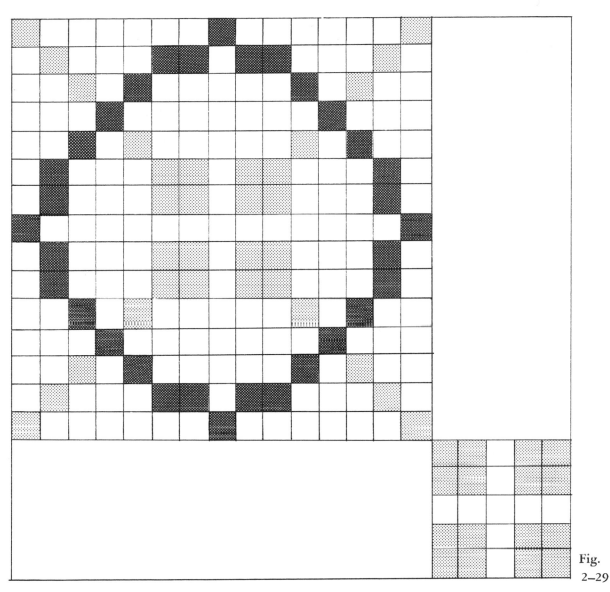

Fig.
2–29

the nine-patch, six little squares of color A and three little squares of color C were cut out. The little squares of color C were pieced so that they would line up diagonally to form the chains which cross the top in a series of parallels. The solid colored blocks were pieced with the nine-patch blocks so that the diagonals of the

solid squares repeat the diagonals of the little squares.

The "Irish Chain" is one of the most widely used American patchwork patterns. It began as a scrap pattern. Each square was cut out individually, often from the smallest sewing remnants. The drawing shows the "Double Irish Chain"

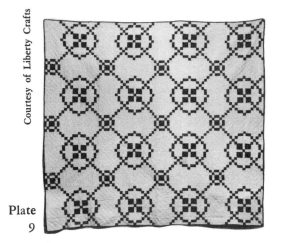

Plate
9

(fig. 2-28). To make the series of crossing diagonals which are a feature of this design, the pattern is divided into two different five-patches of twenty-five squares each. The first block (block A) is made by crossing diagonals of two colors plus white. (See drawing for exact placement of squares.) In the second block (block B), the colored squares occupy only the corners. Block B can either be pieced from squares or the colored corner squares can be appliqued onto a white block. If the small squares are made at least two inches by two inches instead of the traditional one inch square, "The Irish Chain" is a ready candidate for piecing on the sewing machine.

John Burgoyne was a British general and dramatist whose surrender to the Americans at Saratoga during the Revolutionary War is commemmorated in the quilt pattern, "Burgoyne Surrounded" (fig. 2-29). The pattern is also known as "Burgoyne's Quilt" and "Homespun." The mid-nineteenth century, upstate New York quilt (plate 9) shown here is pieced in navy blue prints and white. Red and

white, and red, white, and blue were other color combinations frequently chosen for this quilt. If you examine the pattern carefully, you will see why "Burgoyne Surrounded" was originally made as a one patch. The design was made up of unit squares joined to form the larger areas. This was a utilitarian custom allowing the quiltmaker to use the smallest scraps. Today, with our abundance of material, templates are made for the larger sections saving time in piecing.

TRIANGLES

Simple to fold and infinitely variable, the triangle either as a solitary unit or as part of a block is the most common geometric figure in patchwork. The most popular type of triangles used in quilting are the isosceles triangles which include the half square and quarter square triangles.

ISOSCELES TRIANGLES

An isosceles triangle is a triangle that has at least two equal sides. It can be made by folding a rectangle of paper the desired size in half (fig. 2-30). Mark a point

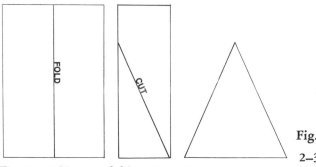

Fig. 2–30 How to fold an isosceles triangle

Fig. 2–3

on the fold the desired height of the apex of the triangle. Either by drawing with a straight edge or by folding the paper, a diagonal line is made between the point on the fold and the corners of the paper. Cut the paper along the line and unfold an equilateral triangle. When cutting out the triangles, it is important to align them with the grain of the fabric.

In quilting circles, another name for isosceles triangles is pyramids. A strip of intersecting light and dark pyramids makes a popular border called "Dog's Tooth" (fig. 2-31). The belt in plate 62 was made from dark and light blue triangles. They were sewn into a "Dog's Tooth" strip, quilted, and bound with black.

"Dog's Tooth" strips can be sewn together until they are the size of a bed to construct the overall one-patch design called "A Thousand Pyramids" (fig. 2-32). In silk this could be quite handsome, but some sort of schema or overall design must be kept in the quiltmaker's mind to arrive at a truely effective pattern.

Side by side vertical bands which alternate the dark and light triangular patterns construct a zig zag pattern called variously "Streak of Lightning," "Zig Zag," "Rail Fence" and "Snake Fence" (fig. 2-33). The impact of the design was altered by choosing a unit triangle with a wider or narrower base. Pieced in bold reds and yellows or blues and yellows, a full bed quilt generally placed the lightning bolts running the length of the bed. The "Streak of Lightning" pattern can be seen decorating a bag in plate 69. A rectangle made from "The Streak of Lightning" pattern in solid pink and yellow

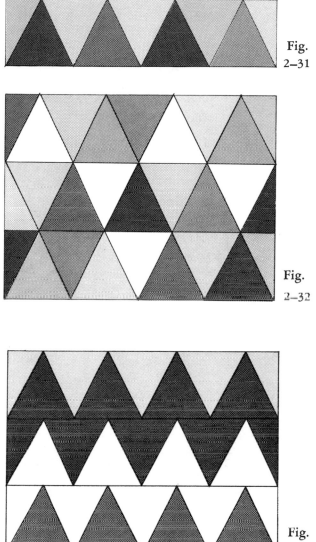

Fig.
2-31

Fig.
2-32

Fig.
2-33

and a peach colored floral print was appliqued on a blue and white striped ticking laundry bag. A perennially popular design, I recently saw a young man walking down the street wearing a patchwork shirt in this pattern on which the lightning bolt followed his spine.

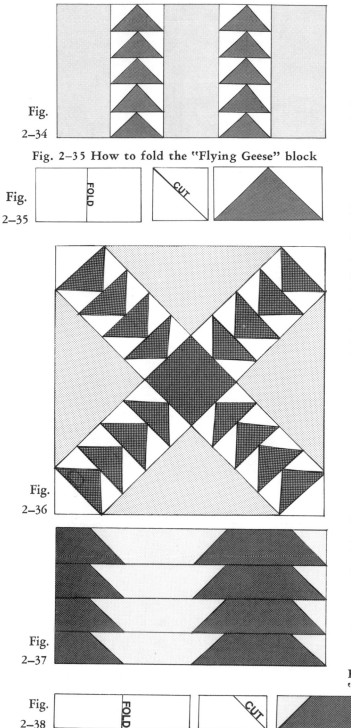

Fig. 2–34

Fig. 2–35 How to fold the "Flying Geese" block

Fig. 2–35

Fig. 2–36

Fig. 2–37

Fig. 2–38

"The Fying Geese," known also as "Ocean Waves" along the Atlantic coast and "Birds in the Air" further inland, is a "stripey" quilt based on an isosceles triangle. The pattern for the main triangles is folded and cut from an approximately two by four-inch rectangle (fig. 2-34). The end triangles that are left are not to be discarded. Instead they are to be used as the pattern for the quilt's end triangles. These are to be a different color from that of the larger main triangles. White is traditionally the choice for the end triangles because it offers the maximum contrast. The end triangles are stitched onto the larger main triangles thus making rectangles again. These rectangles are then stitched into strips the length of the bed with the apex of the triangles pointing toward the head of the bed. These pieced bands are to be set with solid colored bands of the same size. (fig. 2-35)

"The Wild Goose Chase" also called "Odd Fellow's Patch" (fig. 2-36) is a single block that uses the same structure as "The Flying Geese" to construct its diagonals. It makes an excellent design for a cushion. For many years, when this design was used to make a quilt top, the pieced blocks were set with plain ones on which one of the many varieties of wreath decorations was quilted.

"The Tree Everlasting" (fig. 2-37) is a "stripey" pattern in which an approximately four by six-inch horizontal rectangle is folded and cut to make a

Fig. 2–38 How to fold a trapezoid for the "Tree Everlasting" pattern

trapezoid. To draft the pattern, a rectangle is folded in half. A line is folded or drawn from the lower corner to a point along the upper edge about one inch from the fold. Cutting along the line gives a trapezoid. An equal number of trapezoids in each of two colors, traditionally blue and brown, are to be cut. Alternating their positions, the trapezoids are sewn together horizontally until the desired width is reached. Strips are pieced together lining up the trapezoids to build the vertical tree forms. Actually, rectangles bigger than four by six inches can be used to make this design, and the bigger the rectangle, the more quickly the quilt is pieced. The size of the trapezoids and the size of the bed determine how many strip "trees" will occupy the top. In an old quilt in Ruth Finley's collection, two "trees" run down the center of the quilt. They are framed by two half "trees." The proportions of the trapezoids may be varied to create different shaped trees. (fig. 2-38)

HALF SQUARE TRIANGLES

A multitude of patchwork patterns are based on the right angle triangle made by folding a square diagonally in half (fig. 2-39). The simplest arrangement of half square triangles is a variation of "Birds in the Air" or "Tree Everlasting" called "Flags" (fig. 2-40). The example of "Flags" seen in plate 10 was made by a present-day Arkansas mountain woman in mustard brown and dark yellow calico. The jagged outlines were constructed by piecing two half square triangles into a large block, then by sewing the blocks into strips keeping the positions of the blocks constant. These strips were then joined to other mustard brown strips. The quilt in plate 10 illustrates the necessity of planning a design to fit a specific space. If this is not done, as may be plainly seen (note the upper and left edges), the pattern is crudely broken.

Quickly the placement of triangles was juggled to give movement and pattern. The pattern named "Sawtooth" (fig. 2-41) is a border which alternates the positions of the light and dark triangles to form a design which resembles the teeth of the saw. The corners are three-quarters of the "Pinwheel" pattern.

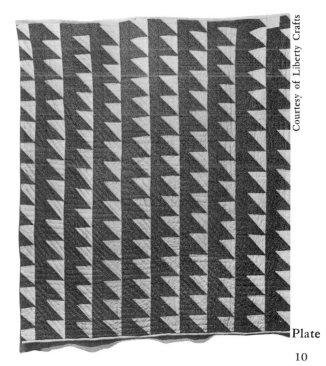

Courtesy of Liberty Crafts

Plate 10

29

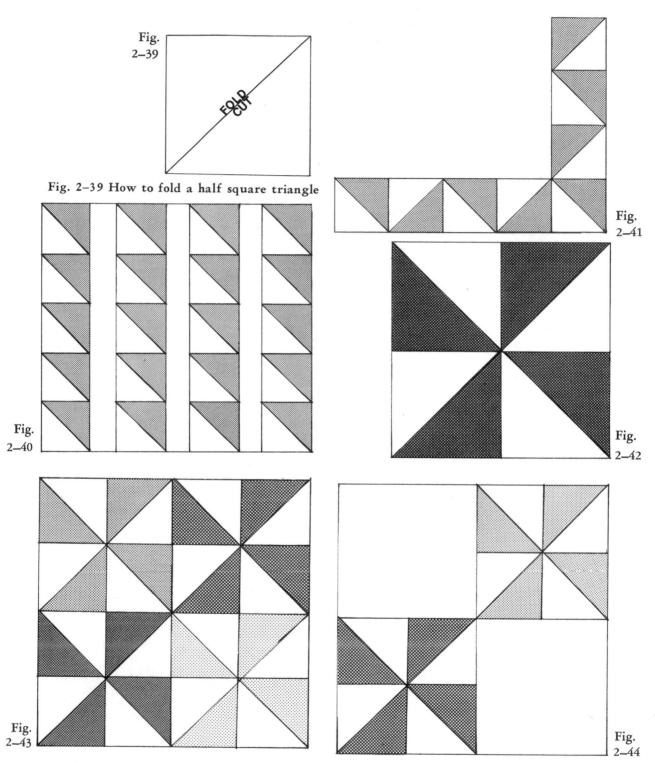

Fig.
2–39

Fig. 2–39 How to fold a half square triangle

Fig.
2–41

Fig.
2–40

Fig.
2–42

Fig.
2–43

Fig.
2–44

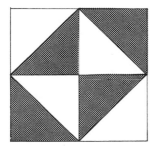

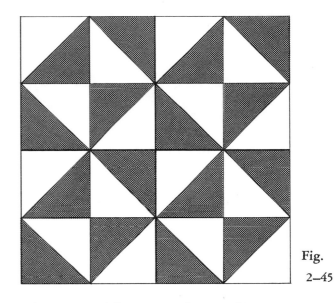

Fig. 2–45

The most uncomplex block based on this unit is the four-patch called the "Pinwheel" or "Windmill" (fig. 2-42). To draft the pattern, a square the size of a finished block is folded and cut into quarters. One of the small squares is folded in half diagonally and cut into two right angle triangles. Four triangles are cut out from dark colored cloth, and four triangles are cut from light colored fabric. A light and a dark triangle are sewn together along their long edge to make a square. The four completed squares are grouped around a central point forming the arms of the windmill and in this position are pieced together to make one block. An 1890 "Pinwheel" top from Weardale, Country Durham, England sees the rose and white blocks sewn flush together. It is edged with strong borders which frame and enliven the central pinwheel section.

Each block may be a different two color combination. When these blocks are pieced side by side, catty-corner sectioned squares appear between the blocks (fig. 2-43). The tie in plate 66 was made in this way. Pieced blocks can also be set with plain blocks (fig. 2-44).

Most of the half square triangle patterns were used on work or scrap quilts. They were called scrap quilts because they were made from dressmaking or other scraps. The top made use of a great variety of fabrics and it was not necessary to have a large quantity of one material on hand to piece them. They were called work or "work-a-day" quilts because they could be quickly pieced and were used everyday. This was in contrast to masterpiece quilts which were saved for display on the guest room bed. Frequent washing and hard wear has made these once commonplace patterns extremely rare.

"Broken Dishes" is a four-patch work quilt (fig. 2-45). To derive the block, a twelve-inch square is folded and cut into four equal parts. Each of the four squares is folded and cut in four again. One of the smallest squares is taken and folded in half diagonally forming the unit triangle. Each of the small squares is made from two unit triangles. Four small squares are pieced to make a unit and four units make a block. Although twelve inches was the recommended size for the block, the dimensions can be varied. The pieced block was generally alternated

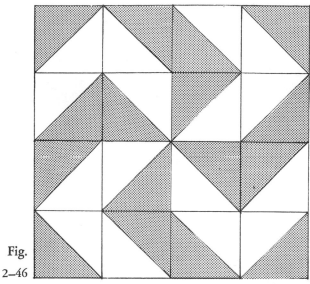

Fig.
2–46

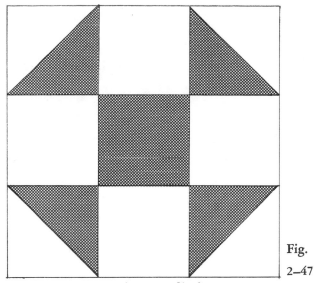

Fig.
2–47

with a plain white block. Each block can be made of a different light and dark combination or they can all be a single color and white. It was customary for the quiltmaker to regard different fabrics of the same shade, both solids and prints, as constituting a single color (plate 8). In this way small scraps could be used up, and in the end, scarcity caused a visually richer quilt design.

Arranged differently, the half square triangles can be formed into four-patch, the "Fly Foot" or the "Devil's Puzzle" (fig. 2-46). The block is made by folding and cutting an eight-inch or larger square into four equal parts. One of these is folded and cut in four again. The smallest square is folded in half diagonally giving the unit triangle. Four chevrons are pieced and grouped like the arms of a pinwheel around an axis. The blocks are set flush without any surrounding border or adjoining plain blocks. The effect is truely "puzzling." The derivation of the name "Fly Foot" is quite interesting. Of the swastika (which closely resembles the

"Fly Foot"), Webster's dictionary says: "many modified forms exist, while various decorative designs, as the Greek fret, are derived from or closely associated with it. Called also *flyfot*." Colonial and early American architecture was predominately Greek revival in style, and it is not surprising therefore that the "flyfot fret," a common form of ornament known by all American joiners, was found as trim on porticoes, eaves, mantelpieces, etc. The term "flyfot" was finally simplified by the rural pioneer population into "fly foot."

The next addition to the geometric structure of a block was the combination of a whole square(s) with half square triangles.

One of the first quilts a young girl was set to make, the "Shoo-fly" (fig. 2-47), is a basic nine-patch pieced from a combination of squares and half square triangles. Named after a wild plant with domed flowers called clover broom or shoo-fly, it is a good example of how quilt patterns receive new names when

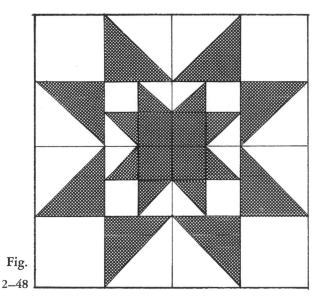

Fig.
2–48

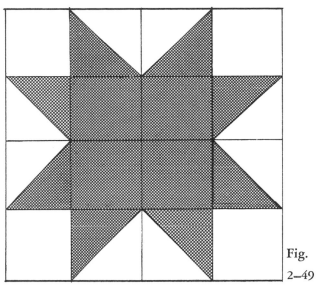

Fig.
2–49

the color is changed. When it is worked in any color combination but green and yellow on white, it is called by its regular name, "Shoo-fly," but when pieced in those three colors, it is renamed "Chinese Coin." To construct the design, a square the size of a finished block is folded in three twice thus forming nine squares. Cut out one of these squares and use it as a pattern. With this pattern, cut out four light colored pieces and one dark colored piece. Then take the pattern and fold it in half thus forming the unit triangle. Take the unit triangle pattern and cut out four light colored and four dark colored triangles. Take a light and dark triangle and sew them together along the hypotenuses. Repeat this procedure with the rest of the triangles. Group the various patches as shown in the diagram. The dark triangles are arranged so that their apexes touch the central square of the same color. "Shoo-fly" may be worked as a scrap quilt or an overall, two-color scheme may be employed. The blocks are generally set with lattice bands with a

square of a different color at the point where the four bands meet. One modern quilt I've seen used an overall color scheme—the blocks were turquoise and lavender calico, and the lattice bands were brown and white polka dots joined by a square of blue and white polka dotted material.

*   *   *

Two of the earliest and best known star patterns originated along the eastern seaboard in the early years of the nineteenth century and are made from a combination of squares and half square triangles. The stars may be made singly, or one star may be encased in another, larger star. The former pattern is called the "Saw Tooth Star" and the latter pattern is called the "Rising Star."

The single or "Saw Tooth Star" (fig. 2-48) is made from sixteen squares. The center four squares in color A are surrounded by the points of the star made from half square triangles (also in color

A) grouped in the shape of a cross. The rest of the block is filled in with squares and triangles of a second, contrasting color.

"The Rising Star" (fig. 2-49) is made in two or three colors from a sixteen square block. The inner four units are further divided into sixteen and pieced into the "Saw Tooth Star" as described above. Framing the inner box, the outer star arms are made from large half square triangles. "Rising Stars" are either worked large with the blocks set flush, or they are worked smaller, approximately twelve to sixteen inches square, and are separated by plain blocks. The inner star may be a different color from the outer one, but they are both set against the same light colored ground.

*   *   *

"Churn Dash" (fig. 2-50) is one of several patterns named after the center section of a butter churn. The sixteen square block is constructed from eight squares of a dark color, eight dark half square triangles, and eight light half square triangles. This design can also be pieced as a four-patch with the light triangles being made from quarter squares.

"Flock of Geese" (fig. 2-51) is a four-patch block that builds its geometric image of geese winging across the sky from a combination of four large and sixteen small half square triangles. The large triangles are set so that their long edges form a strong diagonal cutting the block diagonally in half. Eight small squares are formed from the sixteen small triangles. Each of the small squares is

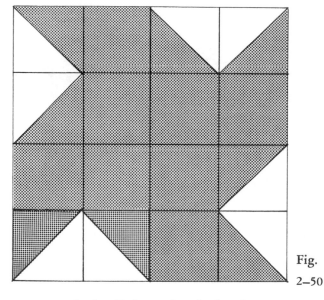

Fig. 2—50

composed of a light and a dark triangle. The long edges of all the small dark triangles slant in the same direction as the long edges (hypotenuses) of the large, dark triangles.

The "Winged Square" (fig. 2-52) is a nine-patch that juxtaposes whole light colored squares with squares pieced from four sets of light and dark triangles. In both the top three and bottom three squares, the right angles of the dark triangles face toward the center, diagonal, solid three squares.

*   *   *

There are a number of patterns called road, trail, or ladder because the half square triangles are grouped to form "roads" running diagonally across the top. The names given to these patterns vary depending on locale and the colors picked for the block. An innovation on a standard block pattern today might even be called "Route 66."

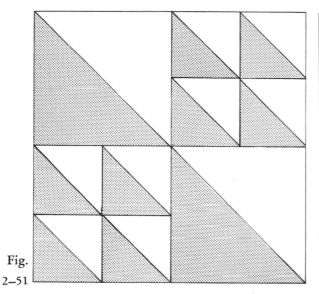

Fig.
2–51

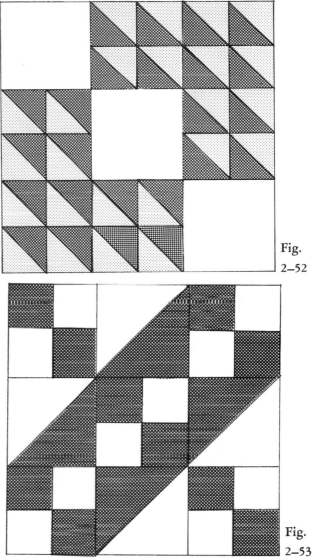

Fig.
2–52

"Jacob's Ladder" (fig. 2-53) is a pre-Revolutionary War, nine-patch pattern made in only two tones. The dark patches had to be very dark and the light patches of an equivalent lightness. The result is a series of "ladders" running up and down or diagonally across the quilt. The block is constructed of patches made from half square triangles alternated with a quarter of a patch square.

"The Road to California" is identical in configuration to "Jacob's Ladder." Its name was changed because the two colors used were brighter and more characteristic of the western landscape. Both "The Road to California" and "Jacob's Ladder" are set flush (without separations) to insure the prominence of the diagonals.

If a third intermediate color is added to the same structure, the pattern receives a new set of names. In Virginia and New England it is called "Stepping Stones," in Pennsylvania "The Tail of Benjamin's Kite," in the Western Reserve "The Underground Railroad," and in Mississippi

Fig.
2–53

and the Far West "The Trail of the Covered Wagon" or simply "Wagon Tracks" (fig. 2-54). Each name conjures up a vivid image of a place or action. The diagonal of quarter squares of a third color are arranged so that they either parallel the line of the large triangles or cross it.

"The Road to Oklahoma" (fig. 2-55) is a two-color, four-patch block. Each of two units are made from one light and

Fig. 2–54

Fig. 2–56

Fig. 2–55

Fig. 2–57

one dark square quarter patch and two sets of small half square triangles. Each of the remaining two units are composed of two dark and two light square quarter patches. In this design, the diagonal of small squares crosses the diagonals of the triangle bases.

The "Nine Patch Star" (fig. 2-56) is a three-color, twenty-five square pattern.

The central, two-color, nine-patch checkerboard is surrounded by a band of squares. Four squares of the darker of the two central colors are centrally placed in the outside band of squares. The corners of the inner nine squares are flanked by half square triangles of a third color.

*　　*　　*

As was seen in the case of the pattern entitled "Stepping Stones," "The Tail of Benjamin's Kite," etc., one specific quilt pattern may have many different names. It should also be noted that one name was often given to a number of different quilt designs. You might have noticed that I have discussed two patterns, both of which were called "Jacob's Ladder."

The labeling of quilt patterns was often a local affair. Very frequently the women in the East would have one name for a certain design while the women in the West would have another.

*   *   *

Trees, leaves, and flowers are generally thought of as the proper subject for applique, but the nine-patch "Maple Leaf" (fig. 2-57) is one of many patchwork blocks based on natural objects. It was made in strongly contrasting colors to reveal the design. Autumnal pinks, oranges, reds, and browns were favored choices. The block takes three squares of color A, four triangles of color A, four triangles of color B, and two squares of color B. The stem is appliqued across the top left square. The pieced blocks are set with plain ones.

Amy Stromsten of New York City used the traditional "Maple Leaf" pattern for her contemporary, photographic wall quilt (color plate 26). The leaves are cut from photographs printed on photosensitized linen. She uses the traditional quilt form to comment on social conditions. Each of the leaves are pieced from a different photograph, and the photographs "are meant to be an ironic comment on America. Rather than showing quaint

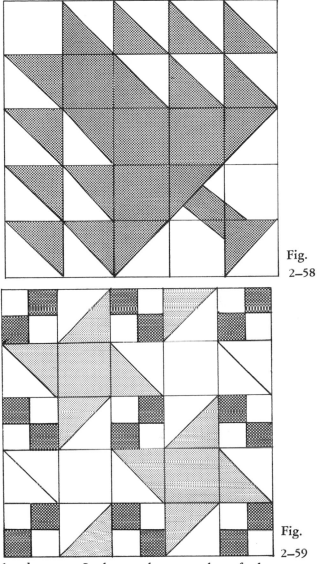

Fig. 2–58

Fig. 2–59

landscapes, I chose photographs of the abuse of the American countryside." The blocks were pieced on the sewing machine from shocking pink cotton and black and white photographic linen then set with plain blocks of shocking pink cotton. The blocks were quilted individually on the sewing machine and later joined together by hand. The entire quilt is bound in bright orange.

The pine tree stood for steadfastness and loyalty in colonial days, and since that time, it has been a favorite patchwork motif. The first flags were all made by quilters, and their hopes expressed by the pine tree emblem were emblazoned on the flags carried by American soldiers in the Revolutionary War. The "Pine Tree" (fig. 2-58) is a twenty-five square block pieced in two colors, usually green and white. It is constructed from the three solid dark squares, two solid light squares, eighteen dark half square triangles, and seventeen light triangles. The trunk is appliqued across the bottom four light squares. The variations of the "Pine Tree" are called "Live Oak," "Tree Everlasting," "Tree of Temptation," "Paradise Tree," and "Christmas Tree."

Half square triangles, squares, and quarter squares are combined in the twenty-five square "Milky Way" (fig. 2-59). Reflecting the source of the image, it is made from the fairy book colors of a night sky: blue, yellow and white. The centers of the interlocking blue and white stars are built from solid squares while their arms are half square triangles. The interstices are yellow and white checkerboards composed of quarter squares. These checkerboards are the twinkle in the milky way. The blocks are set flush making an allover pattern without a border.

*   *   *

All of the patterns described so far are based on standard units, but many patterns are not regular. They use the basic square and half square triangle, but the patches are not part of an equal grid.

Because the blocks have slightly different proportions, special care must be taken in folding the pattern.

"The Necktie" (fig. 2-60) was a widely used pattern for everyday quilts. Depending on the color, material, and setting of the blocks, the quilt could range in impact from ordinary to elegant. To draft the pattern, fold and cut a square of paper the size of a finished block into fourths. Take one of the resulting squares and use it as a pattern to cut out two pieces from a dark-colored fabric. Then take another one of the cut sheets of paper and fold a corner up about one quarter of a side. Cut along the fold. Take the

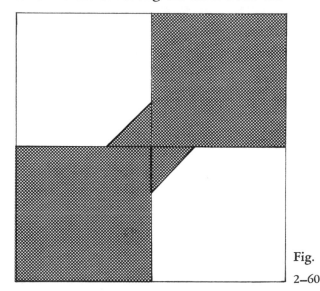

Fig. 2—60

resulting small triangle and cut out two pieces from the dark-colored fabric. Take the square of paper with the corner cut off and use that as a pattern to cut two pieces from a light-colored fabric. The small, dark triangles are sewn to the truncated, light-colored squares. When they are pieced to the two dark squares, the small triangles become the knot of the tie.

The "ties" were made in silk, wool, or cotton. The quilt was either pieced as a scrap quilt with each block having a different two-color combination or was pieced with an allover two-color plan in mind. Solid black and white was the striking choice of many quiltmakers. The jacket in plate 72 was made from an unquilted top in these colors. It should be remembered that traditionally quiltmakers considered any fabric which had a white ground, as long as the figure was not too bold, to be white. This practice gave a visual excitement to otherwise plain designs. The blocks for a "necktie" quilt were either set flush causing the

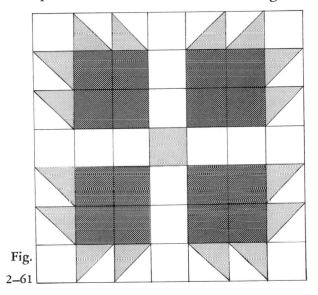

Fig. 2–61

"ties" to make rows of diagonals, or the blocks were set as diamonds separated by unpieced plain blocks.

* * *

The same shape can evoke vastly different images depending upon the kind of life the quiltmaker was leading. On the early domesticated landscape of Long Island, one pattern was called "Duck's Foot-in-the-Mud;" the Friends in Philadelphia saw the exact same pattern as "The Hand of Friendship;" and in Ohio it was called "The Bear's Paw," (fig. 2-61) a constant reminder of the ferocious animals that lurked and left tracks in the mud or snow. "The Bear's Paw" is a **three-color block.** The large squares are in the darkest shade; the surrounding triangles and the center square are in an intermediate shade; and the borders and inner cross are in the lightest shade, often white. In order to make the patterns for this design, it is best to use a ruler. Take a square the size of a finished block and, by carefully measuring, rule the block into sevenths in both directions. One of the resulting small squares is to be used as the pattern for the central square and the four corner squares; half of one of the small squares is the unit triangle; three small squares in a row is to be the pattern for each arm of the central cross; and a grouping of four small squares makes the pattern for the large middle squares of the "Bear's Paw." Thus it can be seen that four basic shapes are used to piece this block.

A shape outlined with "Saw Tooth" triangles such as the "Bear's Paw" is said to be "feathered." "Feathering" was a common way of ornamenting a plain shape.

QUARTER OF A SQUARE TRIANGLES

A square folded in half diagonally twice produces four triangles (fig. 2-62). "The Cotton Reel" (fig. 2-63) is the basic

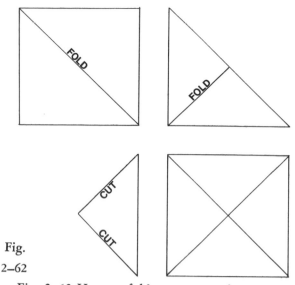

Fig.
2–62

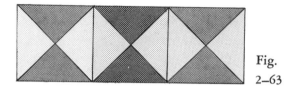

Fig.
2–63

Fig. 2–62 How to fold a quarter of a square triangle

form in which the quarter of a square triangle appears. The pattern was made by placing dark triangles on the top and bottom of the block and light triangles on the sides. The best way to piece a block is to sew two sets of light and dark triangles together along their short sides. Line up the two sets of triangles along their hypotenuses and pin the center seam. Stitch along the center seam and one block is finished. "Cotton Reel" strips were used as borders, or they were sewn together to make an allover quilt. In about 1790 the six Misses Cotton made an immense coverlet in assorted cotton prints in the "Cotton Reel" pattern. The dark and light colors alternated in the adjoining squares. The handbag in plate 64 is made from "Cotton Reel" strips pieced from light blue prints and dark brown and black triangles and bound in navy blue and white polka dots.

"The Yankee Puzzle" (fig. 2-64) is a favorite pattern of northern New York

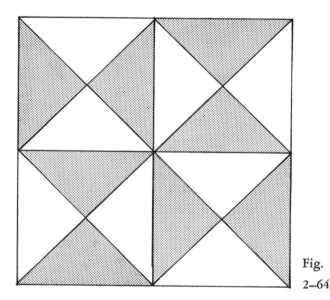

Fig.
2–64

State and New England. It is a variation of the "Cotton Reel." Instead of lining up all the blocks in the identical position, they alternately had the figures reclining and standing to form the "puzzle." When

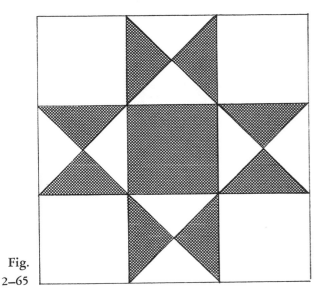

Fig.
2–65

Fig.
2–66

used as an overall pattern, it resembles the "Pinwheel."

One of the loveliest Eastern star patterns is the nine-patch "Ohio Star," also called "Shoo-fly" (fig. 2-65). Around a central, solid square are grouped the four "Cotton Reel" arms of the star. It was worked as a scrap quilt with each star a different color on a white ground. In an old, much used quilt of this pattern which I found in a thrift shop in Westport, Connecticut, the stars were worked in white and shades of figured red and brown, faded by wear to practically the same tone. The pieced blocks were joined with plain white blocks.

A four-colored version of the "Ohio Star" was called the "Variable Star" in the East, and as the pattern found its way out West, it was known by its most common name, the "Lone Star" or "Texas Star" (fig. 2-66). The center square was done in one color, the arms of the star in a second color, the inner triangles in a

third color, and the outer squares and triangles in a fourth color.

The "Whirlwind" (fig. 2-67) is a two-color, four-patch block that combines half square triangles and quarter square triangles to make the broad blades of the whirling pinwheel shape.

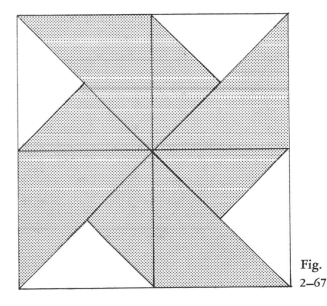

Fig.
2–67

HEXAGONS

Hexagon networks are characterized by stability and order, and it is not surprising that some of the most loved and consistently popular quilts are those based on the hexagon.

Regular hexagon patches were done by eye by the experienced quiltmaker. A more reliable way of deriving an equal sided hexagon (fig. 2-68) is to take a square of paper the desired size of the finished hexagon plus one quarter of an inch seam allowance. Using a simple compass, draw a circle having the same diameter as that of the desired hexagon. Take the compass and place one point on the exact center of the circle, then take the other point and place it on the circle's perimeter. Keeping one point firmly on the perimeter, swing the other point away from the center until it intersects the

perimeter. Keeping the distance between the compass points constant, firmly place one of the compass points on the just intersected spot on the perimeter and again swing the compass until a spot further along the perimeter is intersected. Continue this procedure until six equidistant points have been marked off on the circle. A line connecting the points will yield a regular hexagon. Because you will need a large number of hexagons of exactly the same size, it is important to trace the hexagon on a sturdy piece of cardboard.

The first hexagon quilts were merely rows of hexagons sewn together to make an allover pattern called the "Mosaic" or "Honeycomb" quilt (fig. 2-69). Working this "Honeycomb" quilt was awkward because the quilt quickly became too large for the quiltmaker to easily handle, therefore the hexagons began to be grouped into more manageable rings. These seemed like flower shapes, and the resemblance of the finished top to a flower

Fig. 2–68 How to draw a regular hexagon

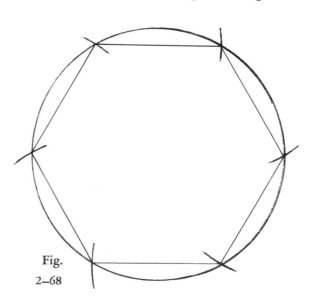

Fig.
2–68

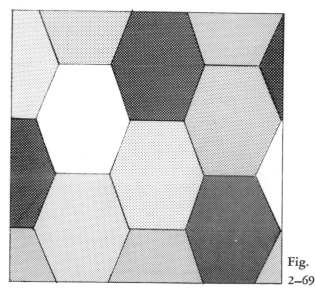

Fig.
2–69

42

garden gave the quilt the names "Grand-mother's Flower Garden" and "French Bouquet" (fig. 2-70). The colors and fabrics used varied according to what dress goods were popular. Sometimes the quilts were worked in silk and at other times were worked in plain or print cottons, but at all times a basic color scheme resembling flowers separated by light-colored paths was adhered to. The center hexagon of a rosette was either pink or yellow. The first ring of hexagons was of print material and the second ring was either white or unbleached muslin.

If the rosette was made with three rings, the center of the rosette and the first ring of hexagons were the same colors as those of the corresponding sections of a two-ring rosette. The second ring, on the other hand, was made of plain or printed green material to resemble foliage. The fourth ring was white or unbleached muslin.

It is important to cut out hexagons carefully, being sure the points are sharp and true. For quicker sewing, stack the hexagons according to color. In order to quilt two-ring rosettes, make a pile of centers, a stack of print hexagons (six of each print are needed), and a stack of white hexagons for the "paths." Working in a ring, sew a print hexagon to each side of the center hexagon with a quarter of an inch seam. Continue building the block by sewing twelve white hexagons around the first layer. When the ring is completed, the finished block is stacked (plate 11) until you are ready to set the blocks.

With this pattern, the arrangement of blocks is especially important, and it can only be decided by laying the blocks out and moving them about until a satisfactory color balance is achieved. The rosettes may be scattered in any pleasing arrangement across the quilt top. White or light rosettes may be grouped like a medallion quilt around a large central hexagon made from dark rosettes.

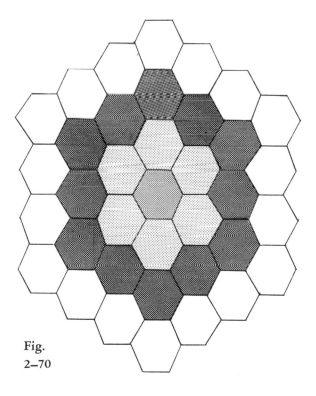

Fig.
2–70

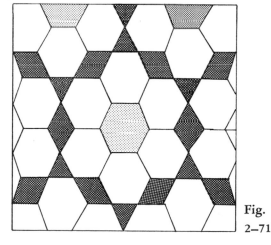

Fig.
2–71

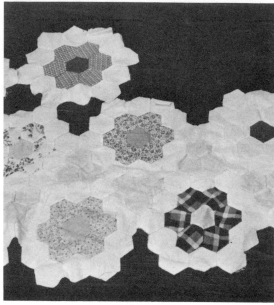

Plate
11

Plate
12

The blocks may be joined by piecing the white rings after the rosettes are completed. The blocks will then share the white ring. If each flower has its own white ring, the blocks have to be joined by a grouping of different colored units. In her unfinished top, my mother employed three pale yellow hexagons pieced in a triangular shape (plate 12) to join the blocks.

Single ring rosettes may be joined with a combination of diamonds and triangles (fig. 2-71). To derive the exact shape of the diamonds and triangles, place three completed rosettes on a sheet of paper so that diamonds and triangles are formed between their edges. Outline the shapes following the edges of the blocks.

A hexagon may be made from a square by removing the square's corners (fig. 2-72). Fold a square in half vertically. Mark points a third of the distance from the fold to each corner on both the top and bottom edges of the paper then fold the paper in half horizontally. As shown in figure 2-72, draw lines from the points marked off on the top and bottom of the paper to the midpoints of the right and left edges which have themselves been marked off by the horizontal fold. Cut along these lines. This procedure will

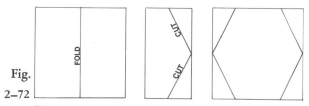

Fig.
2–72

Fig. 2–72 How to fold a hexagon

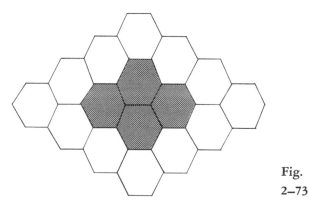

Fig.
2–73

give you a slightly elongated hexagon. If these hexagons are pieced in two or three rings around a center hexagon, a diamond shape rather than a rosette is formed (fig. 2-73). The quilt top is united by the lattices of the diamond shaped grid. The jacket in plate 71 was made from an unquilted top in this pattern.

Hexagon quilts may be pieced on the sewing machine if the hexagons are at least one and a half inches on a side.

Because there are no open spaces or elaborate borders on hexagon quilts, they are properly quilted by following the contours of the individual hexagons.

DIAMONDS

Medieval and Renaissance costumes employed the diamond shaped patch in decoration and trimming. Men's doublets, a close fitting, jacket-like garment which remained in fashion until the seventeenth century, were often adorned around the bottom edge with appliqued diamonds. This may account for the fact that diamonds, one of the three most common patches in pieced quilts, appeared first in American patchwork as appliqued designs.

The diamond was a favorite for making best or masterpiece quilts. They usually received more elaborate and careful quilting than that used on quilts based on a square. The cutting and piecing of diamonds, an exacting process at best, was undertaken only when there was no need for bed coverings. Diamond piecing took so much time and was such fine work that it had the quiltmaker's respect to the point where she could only give it her

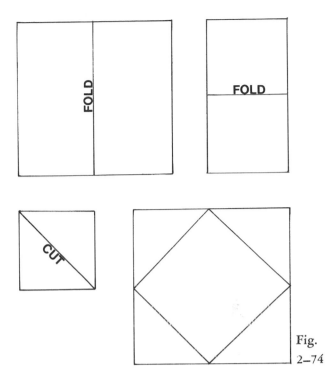

Fig. 2–74 How to fold a diamond

best quilting. We have many fine examples of quilts with diamond patterns because they were usually displayed on the guest room bed as the epitome of the quiltmaker's skill and received little wear.

A diamond is an easy shape to cut (fig. 2-74). A narrow rectangle, the desired size of the diamond patch plus one quarter of an inch seam allowance, is folded in half both horizontally and vertically. While the paper is folded, draw a diagonal from the upper left-hand corner to to the lower right-hand corner. Cutting along this line will give a diamond.

The father of a friend of mine began making allover diamond quilts because he found the repetitious intracacy of piecing the diamonds in rows soothing. He backed these tops with seersucker.

Among the earliest, American, pieced diamond quilts was a "hit and miss" pattern called "Patience Corner's" (fig. 2-75). Its pattern is that of a diamond surrounded by parallelograms. To draft the pattern, place a small square diagonally on a sheet of paper so that it assumes a diamond shape. Outline the square. As seen in figure 2-75, mark a point at a distance of the length of a side of the square outwards from both the left and right sides of each of the square's four points. Draw lines connecting the tips of the square to the points on both their right and left sides. Draw lines to connect the marked points. Using this procedure, you will have drawn four parallelograms around the original, central square (diamond). Cut out one of the parallelograms thus formed, and you will have the unit parallelogram. As seen in figure 2-75, four parallelograms are pieced around each square thus constructing a hexagon. The hexagons are pieced in vertical rows with the long sides parallel to the bottom of the quilt. Rows of squares set as diamonds are used to join the strips of hexagons. These diamonds are to be the same size as the center squares of the pieced hexagons. The makers of hooked rugs in the early nineteenth century derived an extensively used rug pattern from this quilt pattern reflecting the common practice of adapting quilt patterns to other crafts.

EIGHT-POINTED STARS

A much more difficult task is to cut a diamond that will together with five or seven of its fellows make a perfect six or eight-pointed star. I thought it would be easy. One night I cut out a diamond that looked roughly the shape of the diamond needed to make an eight-pointed "Blazing

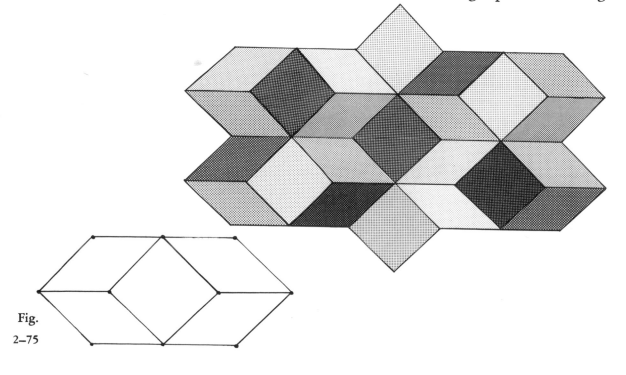

Fig.
2–75

46

Star." After sewing all eight diamonds together I got an octopus-like shape that would not lie flat. The total number of degrees in the angles of the points of the diamonds must add up to precisely 360 degrees if a perfect star is to be made.

Our great grandmothers knew how to fold a square to make an eight pointed star. They used a square of cloth, but we are probably better off using a sheet of thin paper. Take a square the desired size of the finished block remembering to allow for the quarter of an inch seam

(fig. 2-76). Fold the square in half (fig. A) and in half again (fig. B). It is important to make sharp creases using either a fingernail or a straight edge. Fold the square diagonally in half producing a right angle triangle (fig. C). Fold AC until it touches AB (fig. D). The paper is folded again to make point A touch point C (fig. E). Then, using the top fold as a guide, cut along C-E (fig. F). Unfold and you have an eight-pointed star. To obtain eight diamonds that may be used as a pattern, cut to the center along the shorter creases.

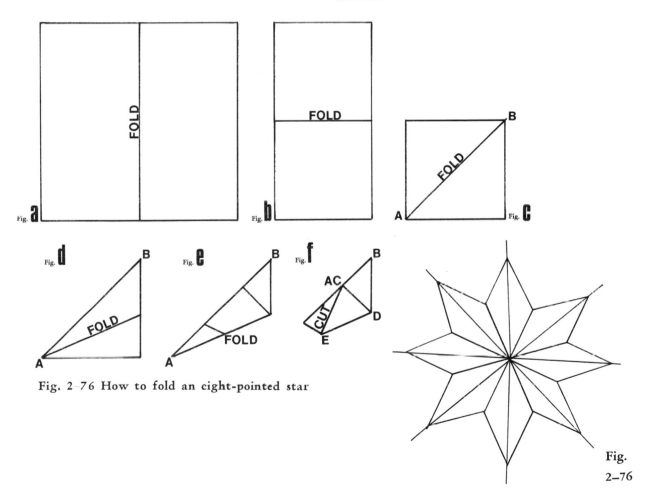

Fig. 2-76 How to fold an eight-pointed star

The star may be built out with rings of diamonds fitted into the arms of the star. No matter how many concentric rings are pieced out from the center, it will take an alternating pattern of squares and isosceles triangles to make the star a square block. The quickest way to determine the size of the triangles and squares needed is to place the completed star on a sheet of paper. Using a straight edge, draw a square tightly around the star. Outline the star, and when the star is removed, the square and triangular completing units will be revealed.

Once a pattern is drafted, it may be used again and again. For each quilt design, place the paper patterns used in an envelope and label the envelope with the names of the patterns it contains and the date you made the quilt. Collections of paper patterns were often cherished and were considered as valuable as a collection of pieced blocks.

The basic diamond pattern for stars originated along the Mississippi River. It was named after the crest of Jean Baptiste Lemoine who explored the river and founded the city of New Orleans. The bi-

Plate
13

colored, eight-pointed star was called the "Star of Lemoine" by the French speaking people along the Mississippi, but by the time the pattern had migrated to the non-French speaking wives of the woodsmen and pioneers, the name was softened and shortened to the "Lemon Star." It is known by both names.

To make a "Lemoine Star" (fig. 2-77), cut a unit diamond from an eight-pointed star and cut out four diamonds of one color and four diamonds from a contrasting color. Red and yellow calico was a standard choice. The colors are pieced alternately to form the arms of the star. Triangles and squares used to fill in the block were often in a light color. Two early twentieth century "Lemoine Star" quilts can be seen in plates 13 and 14. In

Plate 14

Plate 15

Plate 15 Detail of North Carolina "Lemoine Star" quilt showing the variety of fabrics used

49

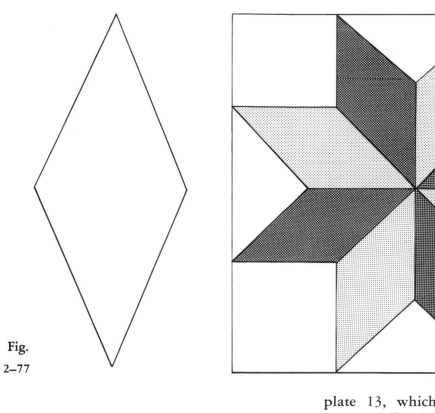

Fig.
2–77

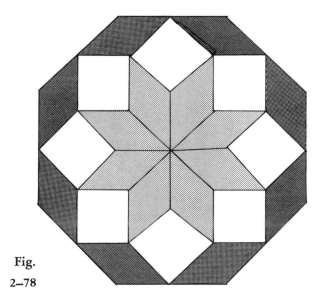

Fig.
2–78

plate 13, which comes from Pennsylvania, the blocks are set with pink calico lattice strips. In plate 14, which comes from North Carolina, the pieced blocks are separated from each other by solid-colored, diamond-shaped blocks.

The "Lemoine Star" has infinite variants, and each one has a special meaning. In a strong yellow with an appliqued circular brown center, it is the "Kansas Sunflower;" in bright red with a round white center and triangles radiating from it, it is "The Rising Sun;" cut in half and given stems, it is "Bouquet of Tulips;" and set in a pattern of squares and arrowheads, it is the "California Star." When looking at quilts and quilt patterns keep your eyes open and you will find many more versions of the Lemoine Star.

"The Rolling Star," also called the

"Brunswick Star" or "Chained Star" (fig. 2-78), is a three color variation of the "Lemoine Star" which, as its name implies, seems to be in movement. The eight-pointed star is pieced in one color. Squares (see description under "Lemoine Star" of how to determine the size of these) of a second color fill in the spaces between the arms of the star. Eight unit diamonds of a third color occupy the angles between the squares making the finished block an octagon. When making an entire quilt in this pattern, the octagon blocks must be joined by triangles of a fourth color. The size of these triangles is determined by placing two octagon blocks together on a sheet of paper and outlining the triangle that appears in the angle of the octagons' sides.

The "Lemoine Star" was the foundation for a great number of star patterns based on the idea of building out in concentric rings of diamonds from a central eight-pointed star. In stars of this type, the arms are generally pieced separately from rows of diamonds and are then joined in the center to reveal the completed star.

"The Blazing Star" (fig. 2-79) is the first of the extended star patterns in which the diamonds are pieced in rows (see diagram). In this pattern, four small diamonds are pieced together to form one large diamond which serves as an arm of the star. The eight large diamonds are joined in the center. The block is finished with squares and triangles. The "Blazing Star" makes a striking cushion. The cushion in plate 16 is made in yellow, orange, and red and white polka dots. You will need eight red, sixteen yellow, and eight orange unit diamonds. The

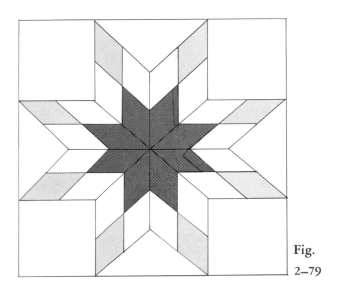

Fig. 2—79

block is completed with squares and triangles of pale yellow polka dots on white. The quilting follows the diamonds. The quilting stitch designs on the pieced squares and triangles were made up of concentric triangles. If the "Blazing Star" is used to make an entire quilt, the pieced blocks are set with plain ones which are generally elaborately quilted.

"The Virginia Star" (fig. 2-80) is a further extension of the "Lemoine Star." You will need to cut twenty-four dark

Plate 16

51

colored, thirty-two medium colored, and sixteen light colored unit diamonds for each block. Each large diamond used as an arm of the star is pieced from nine unit diamonds. The placement of lights and darks resembles the lattice-like shadows cast by an arbor. Eight large diamonds are pieced in this way and sewn together in the center. The block is finished with squares and triangles. Traditionally, a four-armed leaf shape was appliqued in each corner of the block. The "Virginia Star" block is quite large and is set diagonally. The blocks are joined by four and a half inch striped lattice strips.

The grandest of these star patterns is the "Lone Star Quilt" sometimes called "Star of the East" or "Star of Bethlehem." In principle it is pieced like the others but because more colors are involved, it is important to plan the top as a whole. A good way to do this is to make a diagram of one of the arms of the star indicating the colors with colored pencils, crayons, or felt-tipped markers. A contemporary "Lone Star Quilt" made by Mrs. Sarah Stanton of Arkansas (plate 17) was made in vibrant reds, yellows, turquoise, pink, and orange. The standard procedure of piecing the diamonds in rows is followed with the only difference being that the arms of the star are considerably larger. A single star covers the entire bed. The star may be completed with squares and triangles, or it may be appliqued onto a store-bought bedspread or piece of cloth the size of the bed. The "Lone Star" was considered a *tour de force* and was a frequent choice for a masterpiece quilt. (fig. 2-81)

When the star was called "The Star of Bethlehem," it was made in plain or fig-

Fig. 2–80

ured calico in blue tones and white. Each block took sixty-four white and sixty-four blue-toned unit diamonds. Each arm was pieced separately in rows of alternating blue and white diamonds. The overall effect was that of alternately blue then white concentric circles. It usually took nine blocks to cover a bed. The blocks were set so that the arms of the stars touched and appeared to be reaching across the surface of the quilt.

The "Lemoine Star" lends itself to a number of patterns that are at once floral and geometric. A crude use of the diamond patch for florals is a quilt design dating from before 1800 variously known as "Cactus Basket" and "Desert Rose," and much later as "Texas Rose" and "Texas Treasure" (fig. 2-82).

The best way to draft the patterns for this design is to draw a diagram of the complete block on a sheet of stiff paper then cut the necessary patterns from the

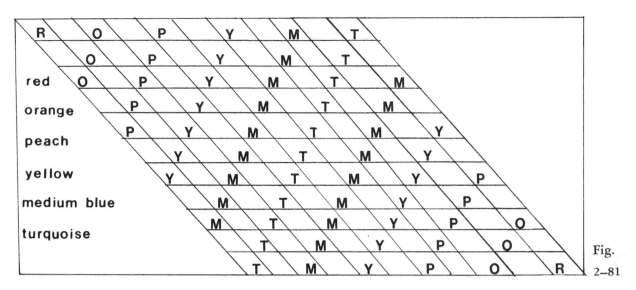

Fig. 2–81

paper. Arrange four unit diamonds to form the "flower" as shown in figure 2-82. These unit diamonds are drafted in the same way as those used in making an eight-pointed star. The triangular "flower basket" is drafted by first drawing a line straight down from the point where the four unit diamonds meet then extending the outer sides of the lower unit diamonds downward until they cross that line. The extensions of the sides of the two lower unit diamonds and the bottom edges of those diamonds form the "basket." This "Cactus Basket" design should be encased in a square set diagonally so that it assumes the shape of an upright diamond. The size of this encasing diamond should be such that its upper two sides are tangent to the points of the four unit diamonds. It is only after you have drafted this encasing diamond that you can draft the two triangles which serve as the base for the "flower basket." These two triangles are drafted by drawing a horizontal line across the apex of

Plate 17

the triangle which serves as the "flower basket." The endpoints of this line should be on the two lower sides of the encasing diamond. From the endpoints of this line, draw diagonals up until they intersect the

Plate
18

Plate 18 Detail of "Lone Star Quilt"

7 Front view of Being at the Forest Entrance, 1970, applique, assorted fabrics, wood, metal supports, string, 6'2", made by Nell Booker Sonneman

8 Detail of Being at the Forest Entrance, made by Nell Booker Sonneman

9 Detail of Being at the Forest Entrance, head, made by Nell Booker Sonneman

8

9

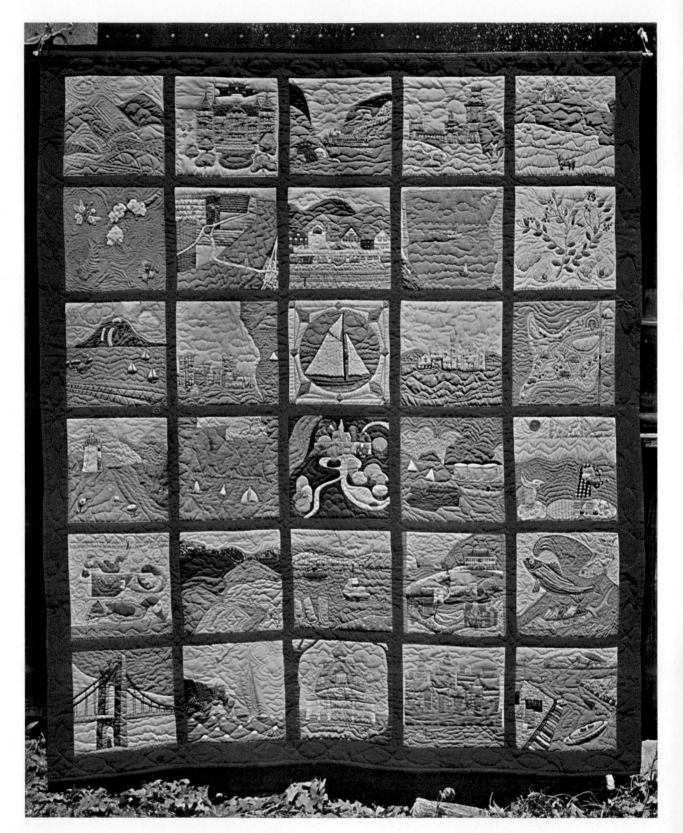

10 Hudson River Quilt, 1969-1972, applique, patchwork
and stitchery, made by thirty women, see page 96
for names

"flower basket." Make sure that the angles formed between the horizontal line and the diagonals be equal on both sides. Deciding to raise each diagonal 45° above the horizontal in order to make the base for the flower basket would be a logical choice for this design. The remaining shapes are determined by outlining the space between the sides of the flower basket and the square.

In the late nineteenth century, North Carolinian "Cactus Basket" quilt seen in plate 19, the top two diamonds of the flower and the triangle of the basket are made from red and green striped material. The blocks are set with dark olive green homespun zig-zag bands.

A combination of applique and piecing turns the "Lemoine Star" into the "Lily," "Tulip," and "Peony" patterns. The flower head is pieced from eight-pointed star unit diamonds, and the whole structure (flower, stem, and leaves) is appliqued on the block.

A half pieced and half appliqued design is made by stitching six unit diamonds together and appliqueing them, a stem, and leaves onto a block of plain colored cloth. The pattern was called "The Peony" (fig. 2-83) by women who were familiar with that flower from English and eastern gardens. The name was shortened to "Pineys." Traditionally the flowers were pieced from red and yellow calicoes, and the stem was cut from green calicoes. The entire peony was appliqued on a white block. When making a whole quilt from this pattern, the appliqued blocks were set with plain white blocks. Quilting stitches followed the flower. Elaborate quilting, perhaps in a peony design, filled the plain blocks. Peonies come in many colors so any combination of colors that suits the room the quilt will be used in may be chosen. One cushion in "The Peony" pattern (plate 21) shows an updated color choice. The flower is pure red, the stem and leaves are made from two different dark calicoes. The design is appliqued on a solid

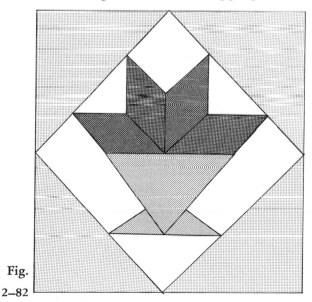

Fig.
2–82

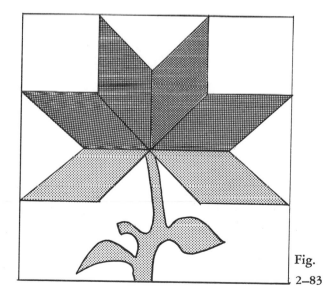

Fig.
2–83

peach-colored cotton. It would be a good pattern to boldly applique on the front of a child's dress.

SIX-POINTED STARS

The patterns for six-pointed stars were more difficult to fold than those for eight-pointed stars, and they also needed to be finished with hexagons unless they were appliqued. Both of these factors made them a less frequent choice. To fold a six-

Plate
19

Plate 20 Detail of "Cactus Basket" quilt showing plate quilting

Plate
20

56

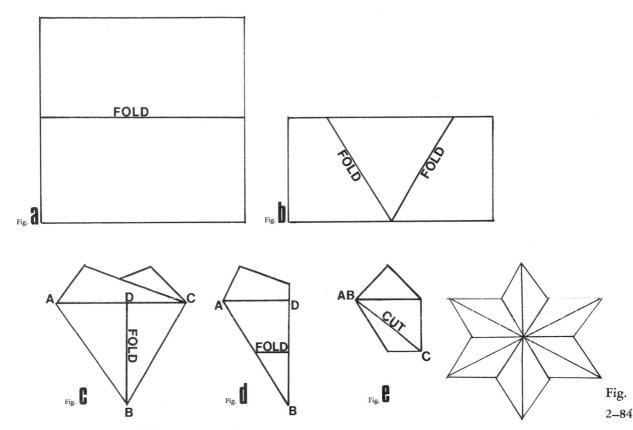

Fig. 2—84 How to fold a six-pointed star

pointed star (fig. 2-84), take a thin square sheet of paper the desired size of the finished block. Fold the square (fig. A) in half to produce figure B. Remember to make sharp creases. Find the center of the fold. Using that as the pivotal point, lay the two halves of the fold over on each other until the triple shapes of figure C are produced. The angles must be of exactly the same degree. This means taking special care in folding. Fold along line BD to produce figure D. B is now folded up to A which results in figure E. Cut along A-C and unfold a six-pointed star. Cut along the shorter lines to the center to obtain six equal diamonds.

By linking six-pointed stars with a unit diamond, a strip is made which can be appliqued around a top to serve as a border (fig. 2-85).

In figure 2-86, diamonds in a contrasting color are pieced into the arms of a six-pointed star making it a hexagon. The hexagon is appliqued on a square block. The hexagon may also be extended to form a square by piecing on four appropriately sized right triangles. The hexagons could also be sewn in vertical strips. A square the size of four triangles described above is set diagonally between the hexagons in a manner similar to "Patience Corners."

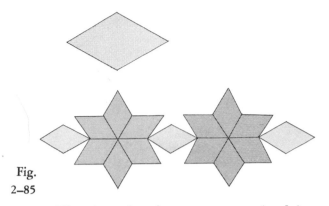

Fig.
2–85

The six–pointed star seems to lend it-self to a combination of piecing and ap-pliqueing. The "Evening Star" (fig. 2-87) is one such pattern. Brick-pink and lib-erty-blue were the colors chosen for an early quilt. The arms were alternately pink and blue. The completed star was appliqued on a block of plain cloth. The block was completed with an appliqued diamond angling inward in each of the four corners. The blocks were bordered

by pieced strips of blue diamonds set with pink triangles called "The Chained Square." The top was finished with a "Dog's Tooth" border in pink and blue triangles.

Seven six-pointed stars may be grouped to make a two-color pattern called "Seven Stars" (fig. 2-88). The seven stars are pieced in a single dark color. Their inner edges are joined with unit diamonds of a lighter color. The seven stars form an equilateral hexagon. The outer ring of the block is completed by filling in the alternately diamond-shaped and trape-zoidal spaces between the stars' arms. These diamonds and trapezoids should be the same color as that of the diamonds which join the inner edges of the stars.

When setting the "Seven Stars" blocks together to make a top, they are set with equilateral, triangular, solid-colored

Fig.
2–86

Fig.
2–87

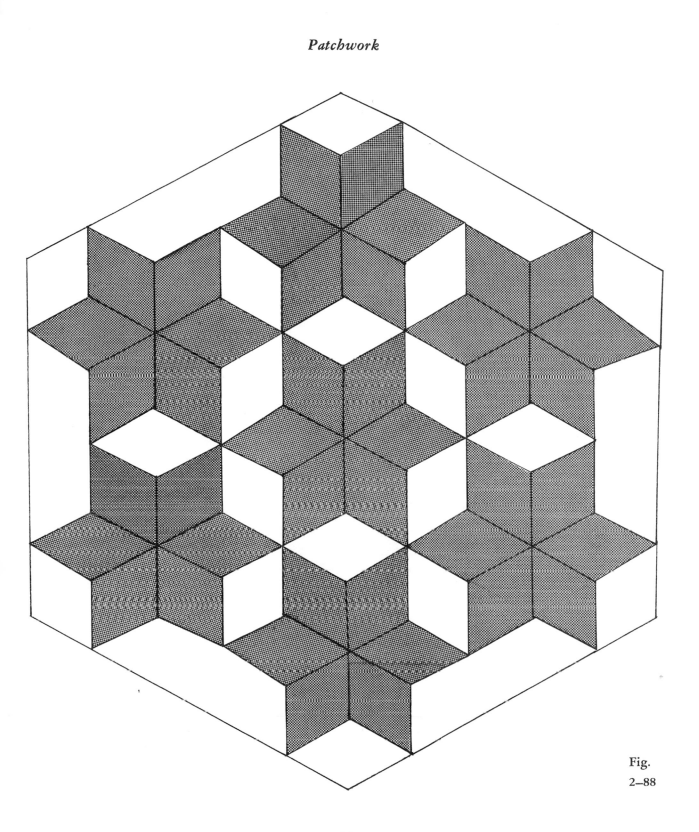

Fig.
2–88

blocks. Each of the three angles in this triangular block would be sixty degrees and each side would be the same length as one side of the equilateral "Seven Stars" block.

Popular because of the optical illusions it created, the diamond was used widely in nineteenth century America to put together a quilt called "Baby's Blocks" (fig. 2-89). The "blocks" were carefully pieced in light, medium, and dark tones to render the maximum optical effect. One nineteenth century quiltmaker made a subtle quilt top from this pattern using only scraps from men's shirtings. The stripes were placed so that they followed the lines of perspective enhancing the illusion.

Another quiltmaker ambitiously used the "Baby's Blocks" pattern to extend the idea of the autograph or friendship quilt. She sent white silk parallelograms to many famous people requesting their signature. Three hundred fifty-nine people including President Abraham Lincoln, statesmen, scientists, authors, and churchmen responded. She carefully stitched their signatures into her quilt giving it both visual and historical interest. It is presently in the Holstein Collection, New York City.

PARALLELOGRAMS

A favorite nineteenth century pattern uses diamonds which are parallelograms in order to make a perspective rendering of cubes. The following method of folding a sheet of paper gives both a parallelogram and a square whose sides are equal to at least two of the sides of the parallelogram.

Fig. 2–89

Following the diagram (fig. 2-90), take a strip of paper approximately two-thirds of which is the desired size of the unit parallelogram. Using B as the pivotal point, fold A over to point C. Then fold the strip along line DC and again along line GE. This produces a folded square EGFH. Disregard any unfolded portion of the strip. Fold G down to H creasing firmly along E-F to create the parallelogram.

A border favored in English quilts is formed by sewing together alternately light then dark parallelograms thus rendering a pleated effect (fig. 2-91). The zig-zag strips are separated from the body of the quilt by medium-hued fabric.

A simple parallelogram pattern is found in the "Swedish Stripey" quilt illustrated in figure 2-92. The short ends of the parallelograms were sewn together to make chevrons. These were, in turn, sewn into strips and pieced until the strips were the width of a bed. The stripes were separated by plain, dark silk quilted with scattered flowers.

One cubical illusion pattern combines two parallelograms and a square. A side

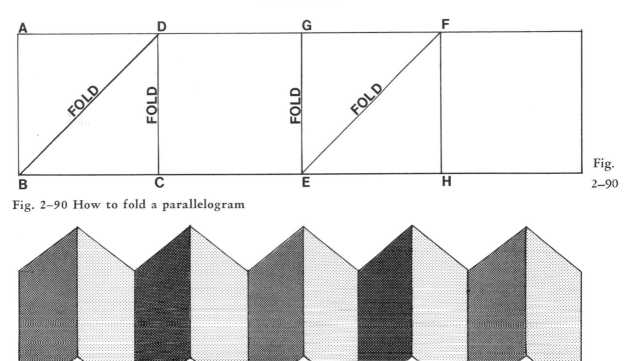

Fig. 2–90

Fig. 2–90 How to fold a parallelogram

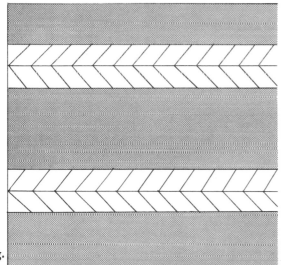

Fig. 2–91

Fig. 2–92

called the "Box Quilt" (fig. 2-93). By shading the "boxes," they may be converted into a flight of stairs. Consequently, the pattern's names were as varied as "Pandora's Box" and "The Heavenly Steps."

THE ROBBED SQUARE

In designing quilts, many household implements were drawn into the drafting of the pattern. One simple unit, a square with a semicircle cut from it, generally relied on the services of a cup or a glass (fig. 2-94). The square from which the completed unit patch was cut ranged from four to sixteen square-inches (two to four inches to a side).

of this square should be equal to the longer side of the parallelogram used (See Figure 2-89 for directions on how to draft a parallelogram) to make a design

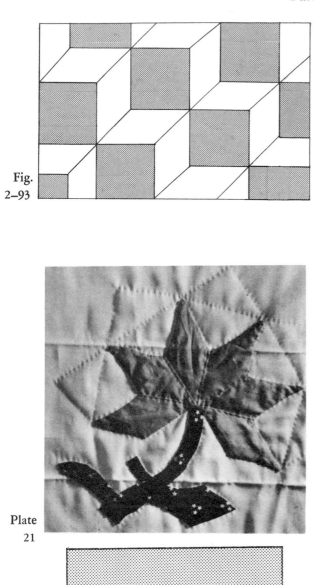

Fig.
2–93

Plate
21

In order to make the patterns necessary for this "Robbed Square" design, cut a square the size of a finished block out of stiff paper. Mark off the midpoints of two adjacent sides. Using a cup or a compass, connect the two midpoints with a curve. Cut along that curve and you have your patterns. This basic patch received endless rearrangements, but all relied on the idea that a "robbed" colored square is compensated with a semicircular patch taken from a white block and *vice versa*.

Recently, I found a fragment of a quilt top using this basic block in a New Hope, Pennsylvania antique shop. It was stitched on the sewing machine proving that the curve can be managed without the careful easing of hand sewing.

Of the many arrangements of this basic unit, "The Drunkard's Path" (fig. 2-95) was one of the earliest and most wide spread, and for a time, it was even called W.C.T.U. (Women's Christian Temperance Union). It was traditionally made

Fig.
2–94

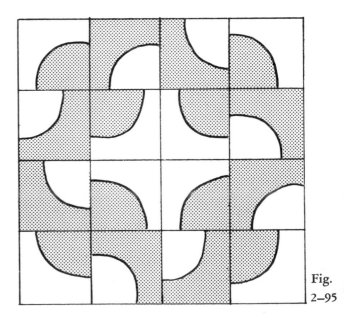

Fig.
2–95

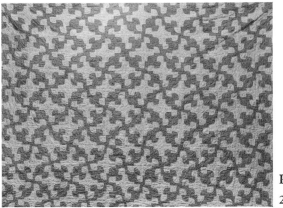

of strongly contrasting colors such as white and red or blue. But color was always a matter of personal preference or local custom. The three quilts of this pattern I can readily recall were all made in the early twentieth century. One from Bethel, Connecticut is a red print faded to rose pieced with white. It is currently being used as a coverlet in an 1860's house. The fragment I mentioned earlier is a willow green print pieced with white. The quilt shown here (plate 22) is yellow and white and was made around 1910 by Lucy Reno Lodwick in California. She had eight children, and after they left home, she frequently made eight of each quilt pattern, giving one to each child. This mass production explains the irregularity of the piecing.

"The Drunkard's Path" is an allover design without borders. The quilting follows the contours of the pattern. The binding is of the same color as the darker of the two colors used. The quilt pieces quickly once the sixteen unit block is memorized.

Plate 22

The other common name for patterns of this type was "Robbing Peter to Pay Paul." There are many variations called by this name but the simplest is a four-patch in which a sectioned circle appears in the middle of the block. "Rob Peter to Pay Paul" (fig. 2-96) may be made as a scrap quilt. Each four-patch would be a different light-dark combination. The same pattern made completely in only two colors, either black and white or red and white, is called "Steeplechase." Both are allover designs.

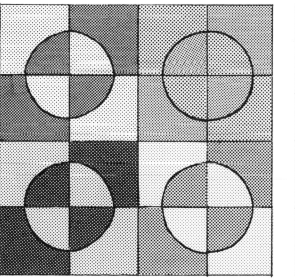

Fig. 2–96

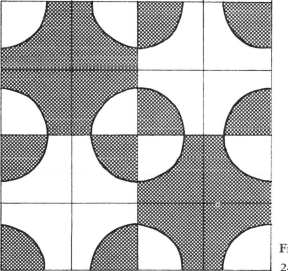

Fig. 2–97

63

Made in two colors, "The Mill Wheel" (fig. 2-97) uses the partitioned circle in a more emphatic way. Each four-patch is dominated by a rounded cross-like shape which is the reverse of its neighbor in coloring. When four of these four-patches are joined a partitioned circle or "mill-wheel" appears. The placement of lights and darks engenders the impression that the millwheel is turning.

One variation of "The Drunkard's Path" was called "Wonder of the World" (fig. 2-98). The three-color, sixteen-unit block features four three-quarter circles flinging the remaining quarter circles into the center four squares. The outer squares are one color, the central squares are a second color, and the circle sections are a third color.

"Falling Timbers" (fig. 2-99) is the only one of the patterns in this group which uses a second unit. This second unit consists of two equal-sized semicircles cut out of a square. When it is combined with the regular unit, the undu-

lating diagonals which characterize this pattern appear.

The two-color, thirty-six unit pattern called ironically either "Love Ring" or "Lone Ring" (fig. 2-100) was used either as a large repeat block or the block was greatly enlarged to make one "ring" which covered the entire bed.

The first time I saw a "Grandmother's Fan" quilt (color plate 17) was when Margaret Gauer Blee showed me her collection of quilts. During the 1930's her family spent their summers in a cabin in the California mountains. The local mountain women were making quilts from traditional patterns they had brought West. To have some basis for conversation, she began to quilt at fourteen. At the local women's suggestion, she made her first quilt using the "Grandmother's Fan" pattern. She remembers, "spending many an afternoon in the screen porch of my parents' cabin sewing and smelling the pines after a mountain rain or listening to the winds through

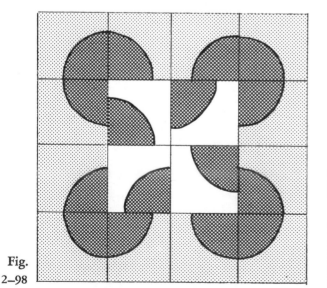

Fig. 2—98

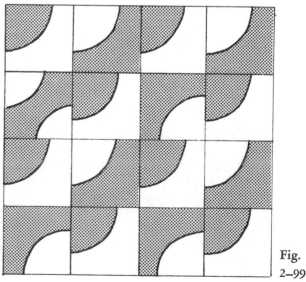

Fig. 2—99

the trees as the thunderstorm approached." She would go over and visit with the local women and show them how she was coming on her quilt. The quilt was begun and finished in one summer. She chose plain and print cottons in predominately blue tones. Silks, velvets, and woolens are also traditionally favorite fabric choices for this quilt.

The "Grandmother's Fan" (fig. 2-101) pattern is drafted in a manner similar to that of the basic unit of "The Drunkard's Path" except on a larger scale. Take a square the desired size of the finished block. Twelve inches square is the usual size. Using a cup or compass, draw a small circle in the upper right hand corner. Using a plate or a compass, draw another arc which will encircle three-quarters of the square. Divide the section between the two arcs into six equal parts.

"Grandmother's Fan" is pieced in two very different ways. For the first method, the cut-out pattern pieces are redrawn adding a quarter of an inch all around

for the seam allowance. The six units of the fan are stitched into an arc. The colors may vary from block to block. The inner and outer curved shapes are pieced onto the arc to make a twelve inch block. The inner, smaller shape is usually black. The outer shape is usually a medium-toned, solid color.

In the other method of construction, the pieces are stitched onto a solid-colored, muslin foundation block. The first leaf of the arc is basted onto the foundation block with a running stitch leaving the edges raw. The other leaves of the fan are then added. Each new piece is placed face down on the preceding piece with right sides together. The seam is stitched through the previous piece and the muslin. The piece is then pressed open. This process called making a "pressed quilt" is repeated until the fan is complete. ("Log Cabin," "Pineapple," and "Crazy" quilts are also made in this way.) The outer raw edge of the fan is finished with a piece of fancy braid or an

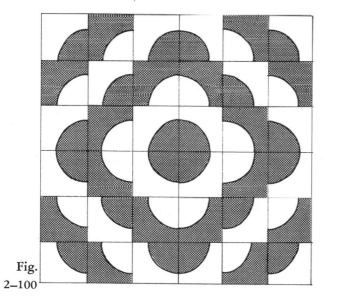

Fig. 2–100

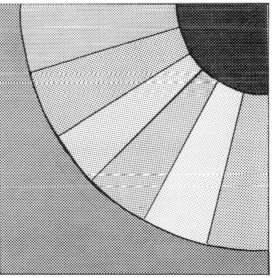

Fig. 2–101

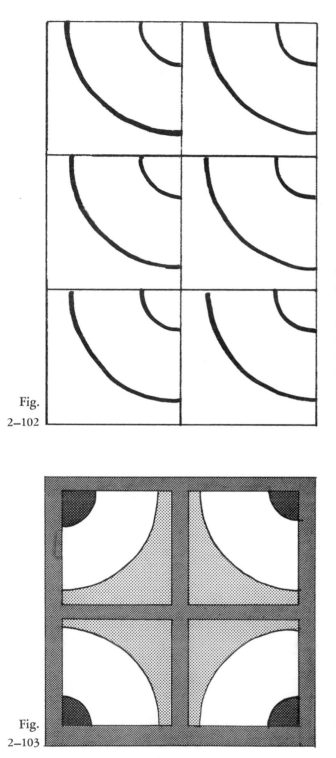

Fig.
2–102

Fig.
2–103

embroidered line. The inner raw edge is covered in the same way as the leaves of the fan were secured. The small, dark, inner semicircle is placed face down on the fan and the seam is stitched through the circle, the fan, and the foundation block. The circle is then pressed open into position.

I know of four ways in which the "Grandmother Fan" pattern was conventionally set. In the first, the blocks are set flush, and all the fans spread their arcs in the same direction (fig. 2-102). In the second, all of the fans face the same direction, but the pieced blocks are separated by plain ones, and a wreath is quilted on each side of the plain blocks (fig. 2-103). In the third, the fans are made quite large and are grouped in sets of four with all of the fans facing inward. All of the blocks in the quilt are separated by velvet lattice bands and a wide velvet border (fig. 2-104). In the fourth and most complicated pattern of all, the blocks are set flush, but the position of the fan alternates from top to bottom (fig. 2-105). This pattern was never elaborately quilted and was frequently merely tied to an old blanket.

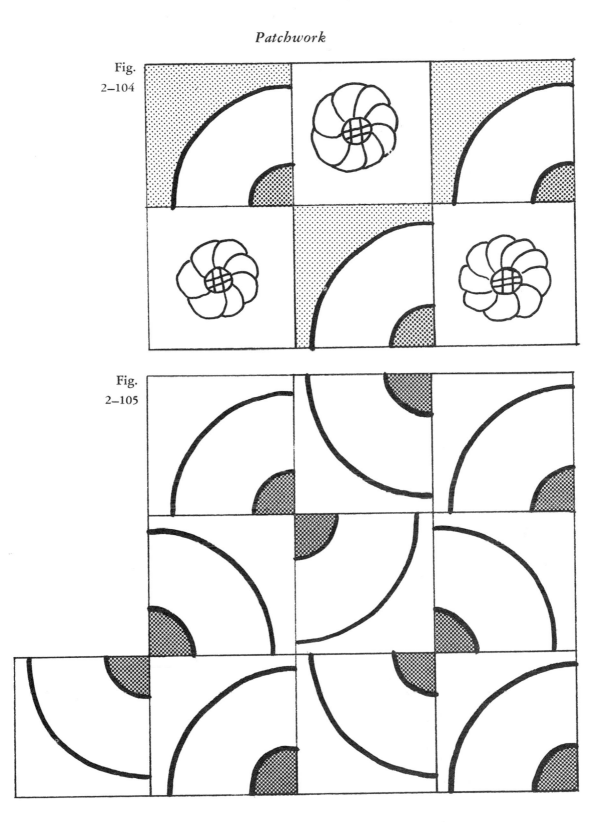

Fig.
2–104

Fig.
2–105

CRAZY QUILTS

"Crazy Quilts" bring the heyday of American quilting full cycle. During the early years of the country, blankets were patched so extensively they practically became pieced tops, and these were probably the inspiration for the first "Crazy" quilts. When fabric first became readily available to make new quilts, the scraps were roughly trimmed to make a "Crazy" top. These were usually made of cottons and woolens for warmth. Geometric systems and applique soon caught the spirit of the American quilters, and the "Crazy" top became a rarity. By 1870 the Industrial Revolution had changed the needs of the society to the extent that, on the east coast, blankets and Marseilles spreads were commercially available and the necessity of constantly manufacturing bed covers at home eased. The last years of the nineteenth century and the early years of the twentieth century were also an eclectic time. Houses were cluttered with bric-a-brac, huge potted plants, and clothed furniture. It was here that the frivolous, extravagant "Crazy" quilt again made its appearance. This time the pattern was principally employed on throws that were kept in the parlor.

Victorian "Crazy" quilts were made from rich, dark silk and velvet scraps left over from dressmaking. They were usually banded and bordered in black velvet. An exception to this rule was Miss Jenny Jones' "Crazy" quilt which won first prize in a quilt competition in Chicago in 1884. It featured a dark, mossy-green velvet border decorated with a waving pattern of rose buds and forget-me-nots in ribbon work.

The richness of the silks and velvets in these Victorian "Crazy" quilts seemed to call for fancy needlework. The patches were generally outlined with feather stitching, but often embroidery covered the whole quilt. Stars, hearts, birds, and even bicycles were embroidered on the patches with silk, silver, and gold threads. Beads were used for eyes, and ribbons were used to indicate the tails of birds. Women vied with each other to see who could produce the most lavish designs.

The turn-of-the-century Pennsylvania "Crazy" quilt seen in plate 23 and which is made in nine large blocks of pink, lavender, grey, mauve, and pale green, striped, figured, and plain silks and taffetas reflects the rise in popularity of pastel colors that occurred during that period. The pieces are small and well proportioned giving a pleasing, allover effect. Light colors did not evoke a great response on the part of the quiltmakers, and it is unusual to find a "Crazy" quilt made in light tones.

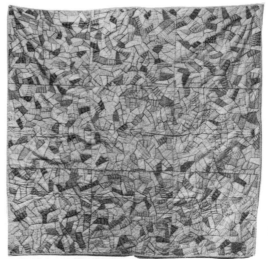

Plate
23

"Crazy" quilts were part of a wave of nostalgia for the past created by a rapidly changing world. They were used to record family histories. In the 1884 "Crazy" quilt mentioned earlier, the Welsh-woman, Miss Jenny Jones included a mole-colored, velvet scrap figured with small, curled feathers to which she attached a slip of paper stating, "Father's Wedding Vest." The mother of a friend of mine in Louisiana owns a late nineteenth century "Crazy" quilt that collages Civil War campaign ribbons and army unit patches with the embroidered silk and velvet pieces. Another quilt has pieces of fabric gathered from a large family. Each piece (which included a fragment of a corset cover complete with lace, a

Plate
24

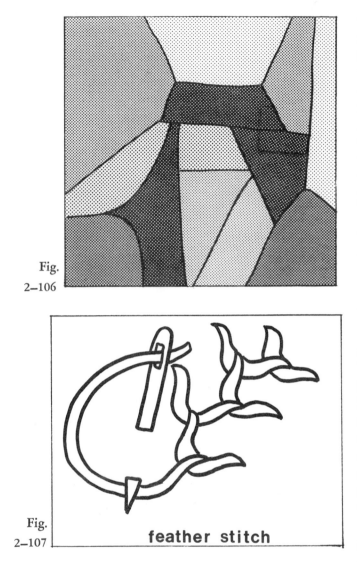

Fig.
2–106

feather stitch

Fig.
2–107

the familiar things of home and asked her mother to make her a quilt incorporating fabrics from chairs and curtains that were used in their house and scraps from clothes they had both made. The center section, the size of the top of a bed, is made from square blocks. The center section is held in a grid of dusty pink strips which separate it from the four surrounding "windows" of geometricized crazy patches.

In theory it seemed very easy to just stitch together random scraps, but in practice most "Crazy" quilts ended up looking terrible because of poor planning. It took a good eye to arrange the pieces so they worked together well. In an extremely handsome, well planned Pennsylvania, wool and cotton "Crazy" quilt now in the Holstein collection, New York City, the designer arranged each of her twenty blocks around a red square. Each central square is roughly framed, in most cases, with two shapes of the same color on each side. The outer edges of the squares are composed of large, dark shapes perforated with light ones. See figure 2-106 for a sample block. The pieces were edged with feather stitching.

It is important to plan the arrangement of pieces. Using crayons, colored pencils, or felt-tipped markers, etc., practice making drawings of possible arrangements. Consider the proportions of the pieces and the color and the balance of the lights and darks. The most pragmatic and practical way of determining the arrangement of pieces is to trim the scraps, lay them on the foundation block, and move them about until a satisfactory arrangement is achieved.

leather bow tie, and a man's hat band) was embroidered with the dates of the donor's birth and death and a line about him or her.

This tradition is carried on in a modified, more design oriented way in Gabrielle Dearborn's "Memory Quilt," 1972 (plate 24, color plate 17). When her daughter was studying in Paris, she missed

A "Crazy" quilt is made on a backing of muslin or other soft material. The backing may be the size of the entire bed or it may be cut into squares to make blocks. A top was traditionally broken into nine or twenty blocks.

When starting to piece a "Crazy" quilt, it is convenient to begin with a scrap with a right angle and sew it neatly into a corner with a running stitch around its edge. The other pieces are then under or overlapped to one half an inch and stitched down with a running stitch which goes through all the layers of the pieces and the foundation block. Continue until the block or top is finished. Remember to use strong, whole, pressed material for the pieces.

The raw edges must now be covered. A double or triple feather stitch (fig. 2-107) worked in embroidery cotton is used to cover the edge if the quilt is intended to be laundered. This stitch has the additional function of strengthening the block. The Victorians used a variety of threads and very fancy embroidery but all this had the disadvantageous effect of limiting the quilt's durability and launderability.

Today a "Crazy" quilt may be made in an afternoon by using the zig-zag or satin stitch of the sewing machine. The pieces are pinned in place, and the edges are anchored with a wide zig-zag stitch. For durability the edges should be gone over a second time with a narrower zig-zag stitch or a satin stitch. If you have a new sewing machine with embroidery discs, they may be used to ornament the patches.

A "Crazy" quilt may be made as a "pressed" quilt. The first piece is sewn down with a running stitch. All succeeding pieces are laid right sides together with an adjoining piece, and a quarter of an inch seam is made through the new piece, the preceding piece, and the foundation. Each just stitched piece is pressed open. This process continues until the block is finished. There is no need to finish the pieces with embroidery because there are no raw edges.

Although a "Crazy" quilt is made with a backing, it is always lined unless it is used to make a cushion. The top was rarely quilted and was merely bound and tied to a backing.

THE LOG CABIN

The "Log Cabin" (fig. 2-108) was a popular "pressed" quilt in England and America during the second half of the nineteenth century in which "logs" or strips of material were built out, corners

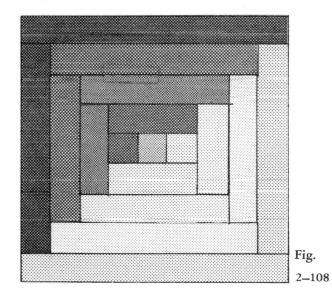

Fig. 2—108

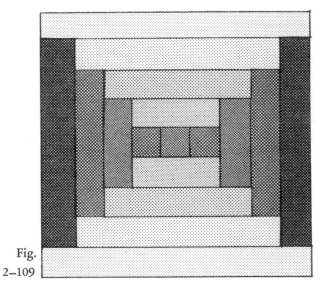

Fig.
2—109

overlapping, from a central square. Patterns were varied by arranging the dark and light patches in different ways. The standard "Log Cabin" arrangement shown in the quilt fragment in plate 25 placed the darks in one corner of the square and the lights in the opposite corner. The blocks were grouped to form stepped diamonds. "Barn Raising" was a "Log Cabin" pattern in which there were three layer diamonds with alternating light and dark rings. The color arrangement of the rings was reversed in adjoining diamonds. It took sixteen blocks to

Plate
25

Plate 25 Detail of "Log Cabin" quilt; ca. 1880

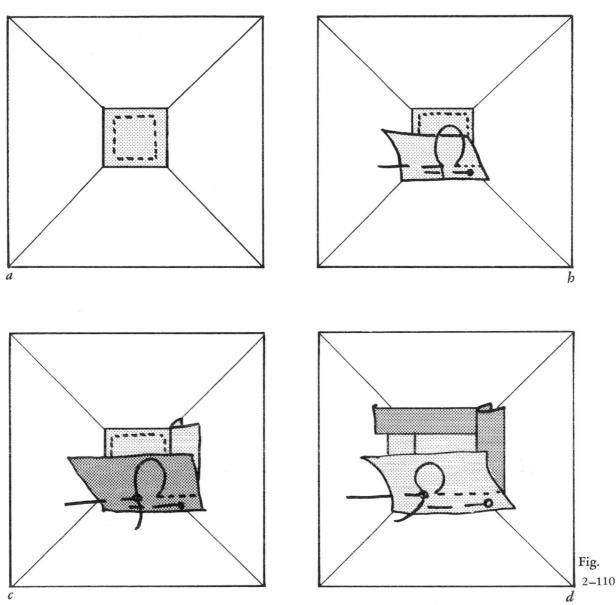

Fig. 2–110

Fig. 2–110 How to piece a "Log Cabin" quilt— a) The center square is basted to the foundation block. b) The first strip is placed right side down on the central square. A seam is made through the strip, the central square, and the foundation block. The strip is pressed open. c) The second strip is placed over the folded end of the first strip. d) The third strip is sewn in position. The fourth strip still needs to be added to complete the first ring.

make each diamond which meant each block was very small. When the colors were arranged in diagonals across the top, the pattern was known as "Straight Furrows." If the darks and lights were grouped on opposite sides of the block, the pattern received the name the "Courthouse Steps" (fig. 2-109).

In the beginning the quilts were made from scraps of print and solid cotton, wool, and worsted. By the end of the century, the "Log Cabin" quilts reflected the "Crazy" quilt fad and were made in silk and velvet scraps. Even silk and velvet ribbons were used to make the "logs." These quilts were called "Ribbon Quilts."

To make each block of a "Log Cabin" quilt, you will need a foundation square with a side of twelve inches (the size of each block varied from seven to fifteen inches to a side). This foundation block should be made of muslin or other soft material. A one inch square is basted to the center of the foundation block with running stitches. Next cut one light one-square-inch square. Place it face down, right sides together on top of the already sewn square. Stitch a one-quarter-of-an-inch seam through the two squares and the foundation block. Press open. Now cut a dark-colored one-square-inch square. Sew it so that it will press open in the direction opposite to that of the light-colored square. Cut two light and two dark one-inch by three-inch strips. Sew a dark strip on the top and a light strip on the bottom. Covering the raw edges of the preceding strip, sew a dark strip on the left and a light strip on the right. Cut two light and two dark one-inch by five-inch strips. Seam as above. Continue as above with two light and two dark one-inch by seven-inch strips and two light and two

dark one-inch by nine-inch strips. You will note that by following this process, all the dark logs will end up in one half of the square, and all the light logs will end up in the opposite half (see fig. 2-110).

To insure precision, cardboard patterns or templates should be made in the following proportions—one inch square, one by three inches, one by five inches, one by seven inches and one by nine inches. If the size of the blocks are changed, the patterns for the "logs" will have to be redrawn in proportions proper for the new size of the block.

The finished blocks are stitched together flush. The top will be very thick and quilting stitches will be almost impossible to sew. A back should be invisibly tied or quilted to the top and then bound with one of the colors in the quilt.

MEDALLION QUILTS

Medallion quilts are a type of quilt that were popular from 1700 to 1830. They are made from pieced work or applique or a combination of the two in which the design develops out from a central motif in a series of borders. The central motif could be a scarf commemorating a place or an event, a picture chintz, or an embroidered or appliqued picture or design. Special commemorative panels were printed commercially for use in this type of quilt. These panels celebrated events such as the battles won by the Duke of Wellington (Vittoria in 1813 and Waterloo in 1815), the coronation of Kings and Queens, and in America, the inauguration of a President. There were many ways of setting and framing the central medallion. The diagrams (fig. 2-111) show several simple ways in which this may be done.

After being out of favor for a long period, the Medallion quilt is being revived by innovative, modern quiltmakers. It's becoming popular because it offers a way of making a bold design quickly. The modern "Bandana Medallion" seen in plate 26 was made by the author in two afternoons. With the exception of the hand-appliqued, orange triangles, it was all done on the sewing machine. The bandana was set as a diamond, and tri-

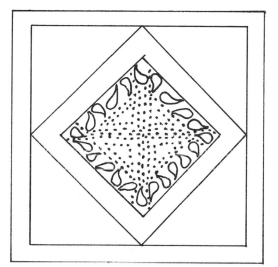

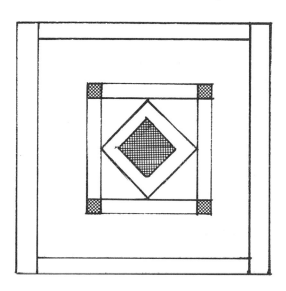

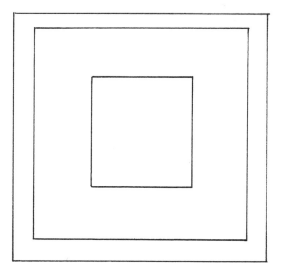

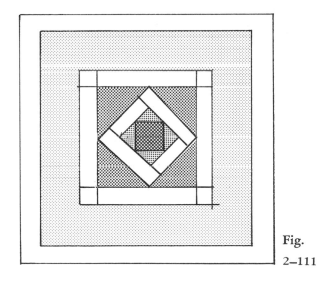

Fig. 2–111

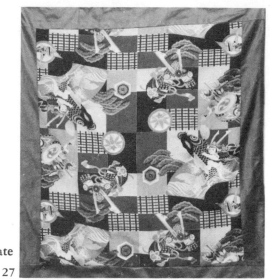

Plate
27

Plate
26

Plate 27 Medallion crib quilt; 1972; a rectangle of Japanese fabric is bordered with turquoise silk; made by Florence Youree; courtesy of Chocolate Soup.

angles were added to the sides making a large square. The central square was then surrounded by borders. The borders were made by tearing strips of cloth of equal width. A strip of cloth the length of the top and bottom of the square was stitched on with a quarter of an inch seam. All seams were pressed toward the center. Strips the length of the sides were stitched onto the square completing one border. I continued making borders of various widths until the desired size was reached.

The design here is centered around a blue bandana, but the central motif could just as well have been an appliqued picture or an embroidered design. Helen Bitar's "Quilt" (color plate 1) is a variation of the medallion quilt. The design grows outward in pieced borders from a central embroidered emblem.

APPLIQUE

The word applique is from the French *appliquer* meaning to put or lay on. The name describes any form of applied top in which fabric is hemmed onto either a plain square of cloth, a block, or a piece of cloth the size of a bed.

The following basic steps will give an understanding of how applique is done.

1. A drawing of the design is made on a piece of paper the desired size of the finished block (plate 28). The design may be copied from an old pattern or it may be an original design. An old design may be either copied by eye or traced. A third method of copying is to place a grid

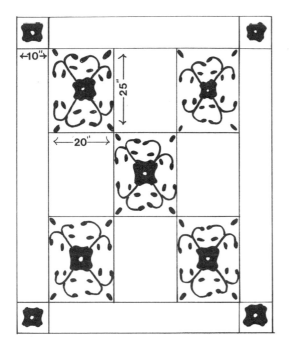

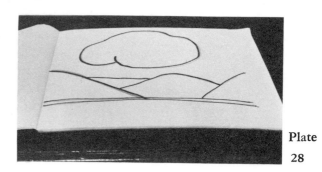

Plate
28

over the design. The content of each square is then transferred to the corresponding square on a grid the size of the final applique design.

If an entire quilt is being made, a plan (fig. 3-1) showing the proportion, placement, and size of the blocks should be made. Some modern quiltmakers prefer to build their quilts from odd-shaped, ap-

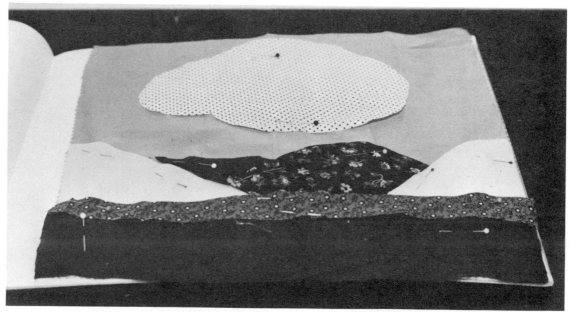

Plate
29

pliqued blocks, designing them as they go along and choosing their final placement after all the blocks have been made.

2. A foundation block is cut out of cloth the same size as the drawing. Traditional quilts generally used foundation blocks of white cotton, but modern quiltmakers now use the background color and material (corduroy, silk, velvet, and vinyl have all been used) that best suit their design.

3. Paper shapes are cut out and used as patterns for cutting out the cloth shapes.

If the pieces are going to be hemmed, the paper patterns should be redrawn adding one quarter of an inch all around, furthermore, the points of stars, leaves, etc. should be blunted by squaring the ends.

When a large quantity of a particular shape is going to be cut, it should be traced onto heavy paper, blotting paper, or cardboard.

4. The fabric shapes are pinned in place on the foundation square. In copying old patterns, it is important to be certain they are centered on the block (plate 29).

5. The pieces are sewn to the foundation square either by hand or with machine sewing.

When the shapes are anchored by hand sewing, the curves are notched to insure that they will lie flat. The edges are turned under and pinned at close intervals. They are sewn in place with blind hemming (fig. 3-2) when attachment is to be invisible. Regular hemming (fig. 3-3) or the button-hole stitch (fig. 3-4) may be used to give a decorative accent. From about 1930 to 1960, the applied nature of the pieces was stressed by outlin-

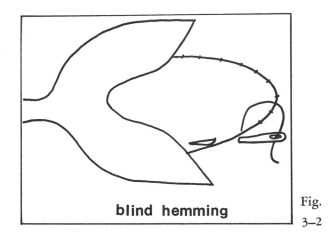

blind hemming

Fig. 3—2

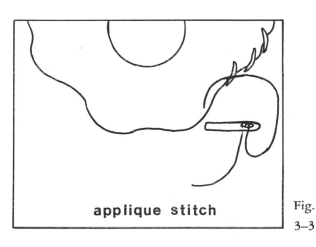

applique stitch

Fig. 3—3

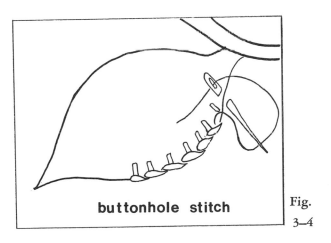

buttonhole stitch

Fig. 3—4

79

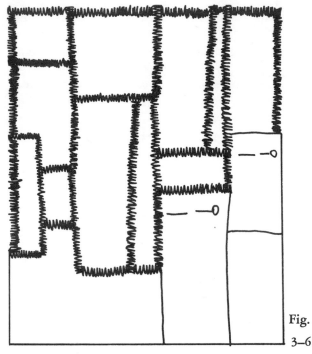

Fig.
3–5

Fig. 3–5 Applique using the zig-zag stitch of the sewing machine

Fig.
3–6

ing the shapes with the button-hole stitch. The dumpy "Sunbonnet Sue" (plate 37) from a crib quilt outlined with the button-hole stitch illustrates this practice. Today the choice of hand sewing generally means a commitment to retaining the purity of the shape as form, and blind hemming is used.

The sewing machine offers other means of attachment. As in hand sewing, the edges may be notched, turned under, and pinned. Using a cording or zipper foot, a straight stitch is made close to the edge.

A great deal of freedom though has been gained by the use of the zig-zag stitch of the sewing machine. The pieces are still pinned in place, but the edges do not have to be turned under. The sewing machine tension is loosened. The machine is set for making a wide zig-zag stitch. The zig-zag dial is set at five and a stitch length of six to eight stitches per inch is used. The shape is gone around once with the wide zig-zag stitch close to the edge basting it in place (fig. 3-5, plate 30). It is gone around a second time using a narrower zig-zag stitch (setting 2 or 3) and a stitch length of ten to twenty stitches per inch. A satin stitch wide enough to

cover the basting stitch may also be used (fig. 3-5). Remember though that if the material puckers, the tension is too tight.

A whole quilt top may be made by overlapping squares and rectangles and then binding them to each other with bars of machine-made satin stitch. The design may be built up as you are making it (fig. 3-6).

The choice of hand versus machine applique depends on your temperament and how you want the finished piece to look. The zig-zag stitch may be too obtrusive for some, but others find the convenience of being able to work spontaneously without having to make allowance for seams a distinct advantage. On the other hand, the sewing machine anchors you to one location while hand-sewn, appliqued pieces, unless they are very large, are portable allowing you to work on them anywhere.

6. The blocks are arranged (set together) and stitched. (See the Patchwork chapter for a more detailed discussion of methods for setting the blocks together.) For small, irregular blocks, hand-stitched seams may be used, but even traditional quiltmakers today prefer to use the sewing machine for sewing the long straight seams which join the blocks of a quilt.

7. Small objects may be quickly quilted on the sewing machine (plate 31). A layer of soft material such as muslin is cut the same size as the foundation block. The appliqued piece is laid on cotton or dacron batting, flannel or an old blanket and the filling is cut to the size of the block. A sandwich of appliqued top, batting and back is pinned or basted together. Using thread the color of the material outline the shapes with a running stitch which goes through all three layers or a sewing machine stitch of six to eight stitches per inch. The presser foot may have to be raised.

Each block or a strip of four blocks may be individually quilted by hand or by machine as described above. The finished pieces are placed right sides together and stitched with a quarter of an inch hand or sewing machine stitch. The raw edges which appear on the back should be bound with bias tape in a color that matches the back (plate 32, 33).

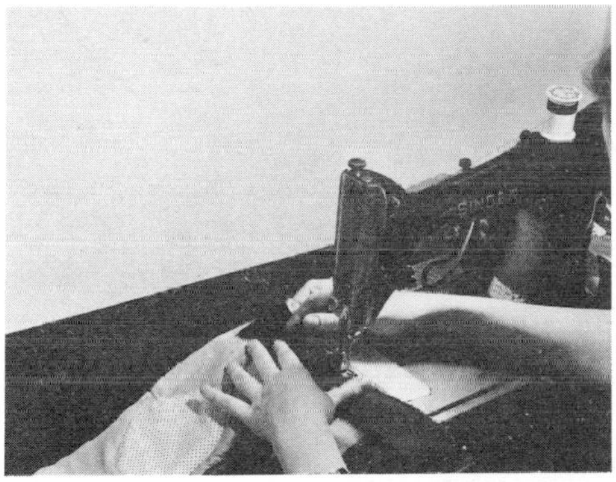

For instructions for more elaborate quilting patterns or for how to quilt entire bed quilts, see the chapter on Quilting.

8. If the quilted object is not being used as part of a garment, hand bag, pillow, etc., the edges must be bound. A two

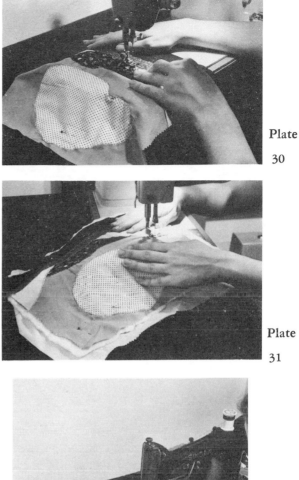

Plate 30

Plate 31

Plate 32

Plate 33

inch strip of cloth or commercial bias tape or hem facing is sewn around the edges, a side at a time, on the sewing machine. Remember to turn under the raw edges at the corners. The binding is turned over and blind hemmed to the other side. See the "Quilting" chapter for a more comprehensive discussion of binding.

Often called "poor man's embroidery," applique is a very old art, and we have

Fig. 3–7

examples of it as far back as the ancient Egyptians. Tapestries were often made in this technique as was the ornamentation of clothes, but it seemed to reach its first real flowering in quiltmaking when the importation of Indian painted calicoes into America and England was forbidden by an Act of Parliament on September 29, 1701. This suddenly made them the most highly prized fabrics for furnishings and dressmaking, and the smallest scraps were considered precious and were saved for patchwork. There was never enough painted calico to cover the then-popular wide bed in the traditional styles of quilt,

therefore, the fruit- and flower-bearing trees of the Indian *palampores* were cut apart, rearranged, and hemmed down on the less expensive white or unbleached calicoes (fig. 3-7). Colonial women applied these designs to hand woven linen. They accented flowers with button-holed edges and softened contours with feather stitching. They called their *broderie Perse*, Persian embroidery.

Broderie Perse can be applied to contemporary quiltmaking by taking any of the beautiful chintzes or picture prints available today and cutting out the figures. A remnant or an old curtain are equally acceptable to applique. The figures are then arranged on a colored or white sheet or on lengths of fabric seamed together to the size of a bed. The cutouts are pinned in place, and the edges are turned under and blind hemmed in place. The designs may be accentuated with embroidery. For example, a rose's heart can be filled with French knots, a leaf can be satin stitched, a contour can be softened with feather stitching, or a bird's tail can be exaggerated with ribbons. Beads might also be added to the eyes.

Appliqued quilts first gained their popularity in the South where wealth, slaves, and a warmer climate lessened the need for the manufacture of massive quantities of bed coverings. There were few appliqued quilts made in the North before 1870, and those few were made by well-to-do women in New York and Pennsylvania who had friends in the South. During the 1870's the appliqued quilt moved North and was made and displayed by all ladies of fashion. In the Middle and Far West the appliqued quilt came to be the prime choice for masterpiece quilts. During all this time, patchwork was being made by people who could not afford the lavish expenditure of materials that applique required.

Applique patterns, unlike pieced patterns, are not symbolic and are almost always representations of realistic, everyday things. Stylized flowers, wreaths, and birds were the most popular subjects. The beauty of pieced work is in its regularity. Pieced work requires great exactness and is often very repetitive. Applique, on the other hand, gives the quiltmaker a greater feeling of freedom. Designs were often cut free hand and display a resultant irregularity. However, even when patterns were made there was a scarcely contained exuberance in the early work.

During the fad for cut paper novelties during the 1700's, the designs were made from folded and cut paper by sweethearts, fathers, and children. The design was then cut out of cloth with a quarter of an inch added all around and blind hemmed onto regular blocks. This method of designing an applique quilt continued throughout the nineteenth century.

You can experiment with designing your own squares. Take a sheet of paper about eight inches square. Fold it in half, quarters, or eighths. Cut sections (diamonds, circles, arcs, etc.) out of the folds in the same manner as children make snowflakes or doilies (plate 34). Open it up and check the design. The sheet of paper can be refolded and more cuts can be made. Cut a variety of patterns and choose the best ones. A border may be made by first folding a long strip of paper as you would for making paper dolls then cutting as described above. Marriage and Friendship quilts were made in which each block bore a different design drafted from cut paper patterns.

The Hawaiian missionaries introduced this form of applique work to the Hawaiian women. They taught them Yankee sewing using small pieces, however, the Hawaiians adapted the concept to the lusher, more abundant life of the Islands and enlarged the designs until one cut paper pattern covered an entire bed. The original colors chosen for making Hawai-

Plate 34

ian quilts were turkey red on white, known as the "pai ula" or red pattern. Later, green and white was used to depict waterfalls, leaves, and trees. Red and yellow, the traditional royal colors found in the fantastic feather cloaks of the emperors were also used.

To make an Hawaiian quilt, make a small, paper cut-out pattern and enlarge it to the size of the bed for which the quilt is intended using taped together sheets of newspaper or wrapping paper. Fold the applique material in the same way as the paper pattern. Pin the folded paper pattern on the folded cloth and cut

Fig.
3—8

Fig. 3—8 "The Whig Rose"

Fig.
3—9

Fig. 3—9 "Oak Leaf Wreath"

out adding one eighth of an inch all around. The cut cloth shape is pinned to a piece of cloth the size of the bed. The edges are pinned under and blind hemmed in place. The quilting was built out in equally spaced lines from the contours of the applique. This was called *luma-lau*, wave quilting.

* * *

Gradually standard applique patterns such as "The Whig Rose," "The Oak Leaf Wreath," and "The Ohio Rose" developed. Household implements were used in the drafting of these patterns. Tea cups could be easily manipulated for tracing oval leaf shapes. Smaller circular objects such as spools or salt cellars were just the right size for outlining cherries or grapes. The fancy, fluted cookie cutters and butter stamps popular during the first three-quarters of the nineteenth century were, as Ruth Finley put it, "useful to the needlewoman as well as the cook." Some-

times the objects depicted seem to have been merely traced from the real thing such as the oak leaves in "The Oak Leaf Wreath" or in another case, a potato masher is distinctly visible in the pendants of a border. (figs. 3-8, 3-9, 3-10)

An unfinished block, a variation of "The Oak Leaf" pattern, found in a little hair trunk in a Huntington, Long Island attic in 1927 illustrates the traditional method of applique. Although the block is crumbling, yellow basting threads (a different color from the design was used to provide contrast) about a half an inch from the edge of the appliqued leaves hold the turkey red leaves to the stained white cotton. The next step would have been to turn the edges under and hem them to the block, but a needle is rusted in the corner and the block is unfinished.

Ruth Finley told its story. The block belong to "a beautiful, self-willed girl who was particularly fond of water and all things pertaining to it." The inhabitants of Long Island in the old days were

Fig. 3–10

Fig. 3–10 "Ohio Rose," "Rose of Sharon," or "California Rose"

divided into two classes, those who went to sea in ships and those who did not. The young woman's parents would have nothing to do with those who went to sea. The girl, however, loved a handsome whaling captain. In order to stop the romance, the father told the captain never to come to the house again. The captain though with her "vow of love ringing in his ears, had flung himself out the door, swearing with all the vividness of a sailor's language that he'd marry his sweetheart despite any and all." Her father, as was considered proper in 1828, locked his daughter in her room where she worked on the block. After two weeks she gave in and agreed to marry the village gentleman of her parent's choice. The newly engaged couple went clamming, a favorite Long Island sport. While the clams were cooking, a sailing vessel dropped anchor. A dory manned by several strong sailors skimmed to shore. A crowd of young people moved to meet it when suddenly the captain ap-

peared and grabbed the girl in his arms and eloped with her under their noses in an open boat. An eyewitness said, "The setting sun made a path of gold straight from the beach to the waiting ship, and that the dory followed it, the young woman on the stern seat with her lover's arm around her laughing and kissing her hands to the shore."

If you trace the shapes given in figure 3-11, remembering to add one quarter of an inch seam allowance, you can make your own "Oak Leaf Wreath" quilt. You will need five yards of 72-inch sheeting and three yards of red print. Cut sixteen sixteen-and-one-half-inch-square pieces from the sheeting. The rest of the sheeting will make fifteen-inch wide strips which will border the central appliqued blocks. Trace the full-size patterns, adding one quarter of an inch all around. Using carbon paper, transfer the pattern to cardboard. The paper patterns may also be cut out and traced on cardboard. Cut sixteen centers, sixty-four oak leaves and sixty-four scallops. Stack the cut out pieces according to kind. Pin according to the diagram, turn under the edges, and hem. The completed squares are sewn together four across in both width and length. A fifteen inch wide border is sewn around the appliqued blocks.

The "Ohio Rose" (also called "The California Rose" and "The Rose of Sharon") was another popular pattern. A quilt in this pattern (plate 35) made in the traditional red and green wreaths appliqued on white was found folded in a drawer in upstate New York. Though it probably dates from before 1850, it has hardly been used. The quilt design is made of two units. The twelve central

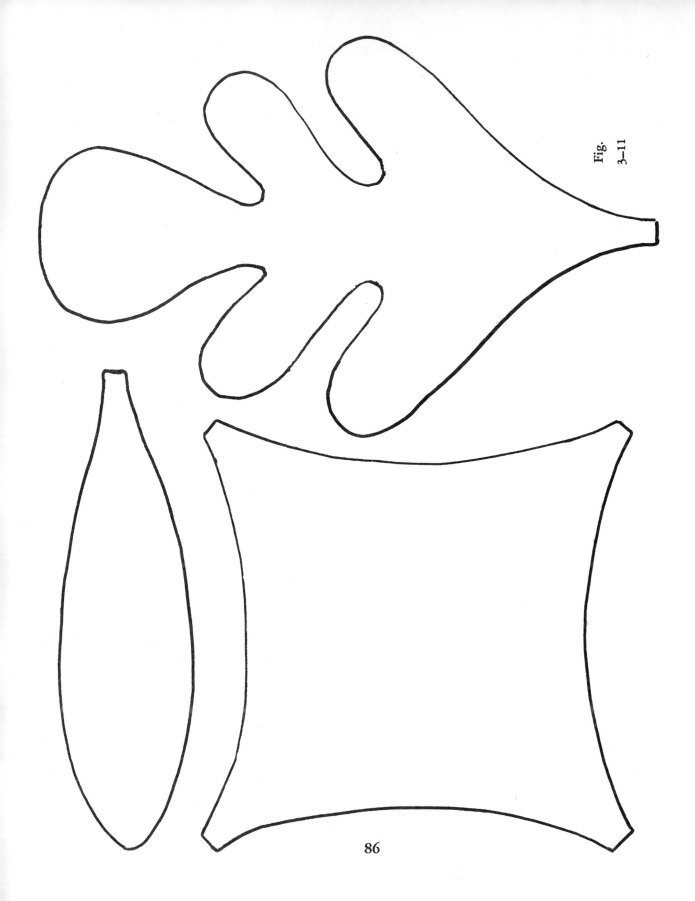

Fig.
3–11

13

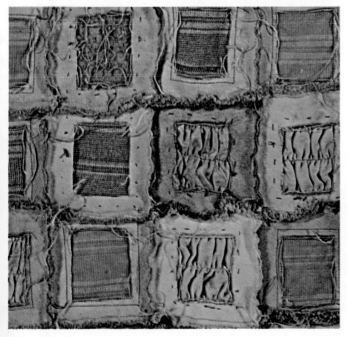

11 Saw Toothed Star Pillow, 1972, made by Jane Lyons and Phyllis Luberg

12 Detail of Remade Block Blanket, 1972, canvas, wool, rayon, cotton—dyed and stitched, 8' x 6', made by Bonnie Gisel

13 Pillow, 1972, made by Phyllis Luberg and Jane Lyons

14 Quilt, satin stitched emblems, made by Helen Bitar

14

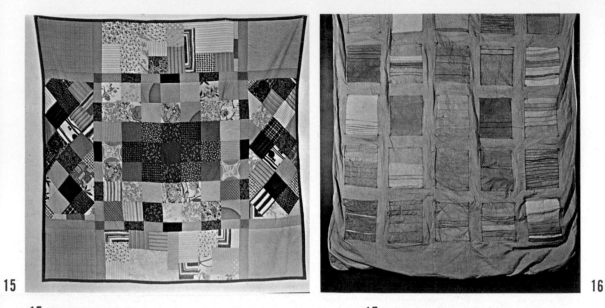

15 Memory Quilt, 1971, made by Gabrielle Dearborn

16 Pink and Blue Quilt, 1971, canvas stitched and dyed, 9' x 7', made by Bonnie Gisel

17 Grandmother's Fan, early 1930's, made by Margaret Gauer Blee

18 Sun Bonnet Sue, made by Margaret Gauer Blee

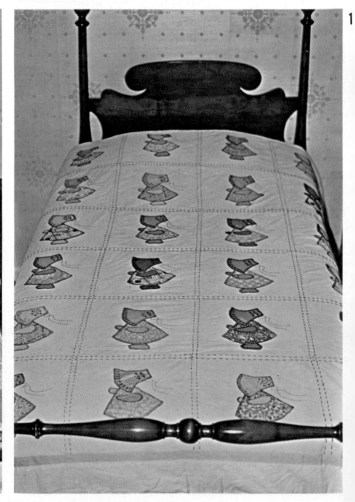

shapes each consisted of four red roses surrounded by green leaves. These are grouped around a red and green, indented, square center. The outer eighteen blocks each had three roses radiating from a smaller all red center.

Most applique patterns you will find in books, magazines, or the library will not be to scale and ready to cut out. You will need to learn how to transfer and enlarge patterns. The best method for doing this is gridding. Because of its simple contours, "The Ohio Rose" is a good pattern to practice on (fig. 3-10).

1. First draw a plan of the quilt top indicating the size of the blocks and the dimensions of the border.

2. Using a ruler and a right angle, draw a grid of one inch or smaller

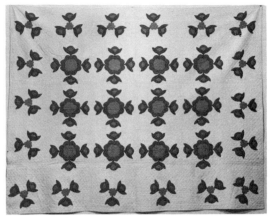

Plate 35

squares on top of the design. Bear in mind that the more detailed the drawing, the smaller these squares should be. If the design is in a book, paper clip a sheet of tracing paper over the page and with a soft marking instrument, grid as above.

Plate 36 Detail of "Ohio Rose" quilt showing the quilting stitches

Plate 36

87

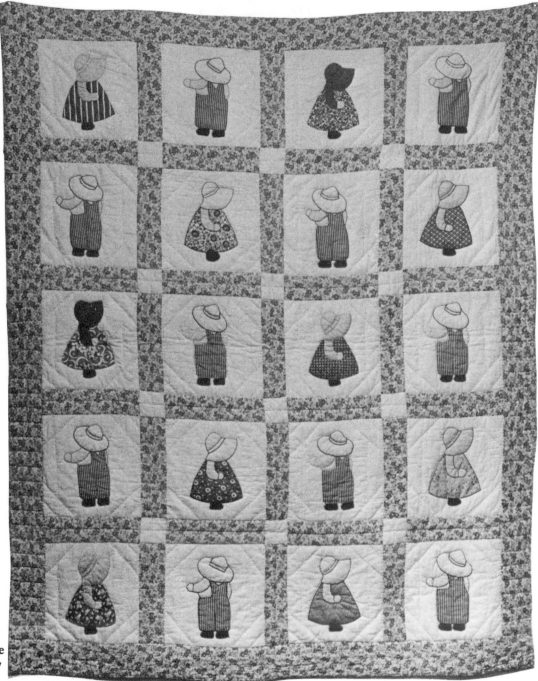

Plate
37

Sunbonnet Sue and Farmer Boy Quilt, North Carolina,
made from hand picked and hand loomed cotton, owned
by Phyllis Luberg and Jane Lyons

Detail of Sunbonnet Sue and Farmer Boy quilt

Plate
39

Detail of a contemporary Sunbonnet Sue crib quilt—The
figure is outlined with the button hole stitch

89

3. Take a sheet of paper the size desired for the finished block and grid it with the same number of lines as you have the small design. They will be proportionately larger.

4. Transfer the design within each original square to the corresponding square in the larger drawing. It is sometimes easier to number the horizontal and vertical columns on both grids in order to keep track of which square is being copied.

5. Cut out the shapes. Trace these shapes on cardboard adding a one-quarter-of-an-inch seam allowance then proceed in the regular steps of appliqueing a design.

ESTIMATING YARDAGE

Another problem you'll face in drafting your own patterns is estimating yardage. To make a proper estimation, first determine the size of the quilt. (See

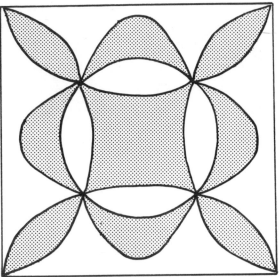

Fig. 3–13

Fig. 3–13 "The Reel"

Patchwork chapter for more detailed instructions.) That much material plus about six inches added to both the length and width for the seams is bought for the foundation of the top.

If scraps are used for the appliqued sections, it is not necessary to estimate yardage for the design, but if the pattern calls for a definite, allover color scheme such as the red, green, and white of "The Ohio Rose" pattern, one must know how much material should be purchased.

One method of material estimation measures each shape as if it were a square. A flower with a one-inch diameter center, a two-inch inner circle of petals, and a three-inch outer circle of leaves would need a piece of cloth 3½ inches wide by 7½ inches long if all three pieces were to be cut from one color of material.

Another method is simpler but less accurate. If the top is appliqued in one color, it takes approximately six yards of thirty-six-inch-wide material. If the design has more than one color, make a

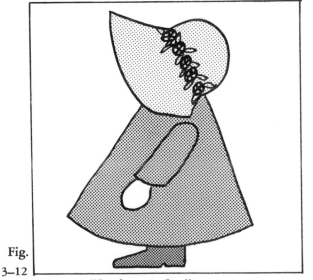

Fig. 3–12

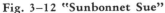

Fig. 3–12 "Sunbonnet Sue"

90

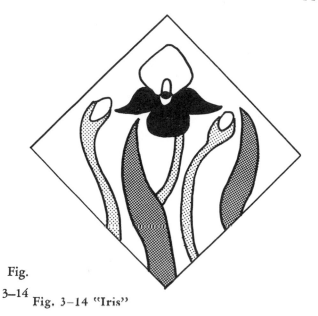

Fig.
3–14   Fig. 3–14 "Iris"

Margaret Gauer Blee's quilt (color plate 17) shows the standard rendition of the pattern. Twenty-four "Sunbonnet Sues" all facing in the same direction, all wearing identical poke bonnets and full skirts, varying only in color are appliqued on white blocks. The quilt is bound in light blue. This exact pattern appears across the United States.

The epitome of this design is reached in a North Carolinian quilt made from cotton picked and hand loomed by the quiltmaker (plate 37). The blocks are alternately a boy wearing a round straw hat and blue and white striped overalls facing away with one arm extended and a girl in a poke bonnet facing sideways (plate 38). The appliqued squares are set in a purple on white, small, floral print meeting at pink squares. The quilt is backed with the same open woven cotton print. The proportions of the figures are excellent. The deft use of a boy and a girl and the appropriate choice of materials makes this an outstanding quilt.

rough estimate of the proportion of the design each color occupies then divide into six yards to arrive at the correct yardage. If the design is divided into equal amounts of two colors then three yards of each color would be needed. If two-thirds of the design were green and one third was red, as in "The Ohio Rose," four yards of green cloth and two yards of red cloth would be required.

*   *   *

Rigid traditions soon surrounded appliqued quilt designs. By the late nineteenth and early twentieth century the designs became codified and endlessly repeated with only slight variations. Stamped blocks and patterns were sold. One example of this is the "Sunbonnet Sue" (fig. 3-12) which was extremely popular from 1930 to 1960 and made by all types of women. The following three quilts in this design show how a standard pattern can be varied.

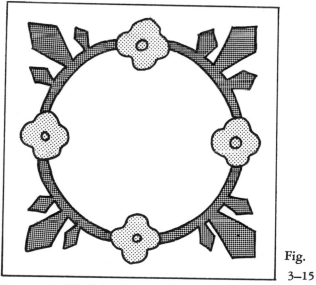

Fig.
3–15

Fig. 3–15 "Hollyhock Wreath"

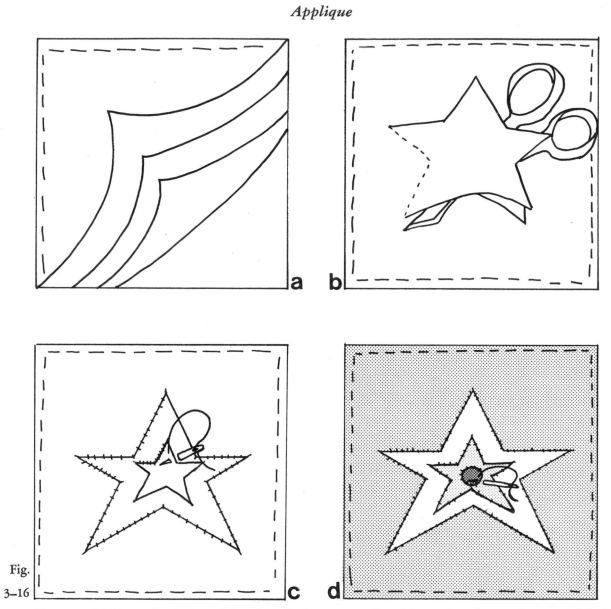

Fig.
3–16

Fig. 3–16 Making a "mola"— a) basting the layers together; b) cutting the top layer; c) blind hemming the design; d) successive layers are cut and hemmed

The nadir of the design is found in a recent crib quilt (plate 39). The quilt features twelve lumpy, irregular "Sunbonnet Sues" outlined with button-hole stitches. Ironically, though, it displays a kind of primitiveness which gives it a vigor that the first quilt which exhibits better workmanship does not have.

*   *   *

Applique as a means of picture making has a long, American folk art tradition. Harriet Power's "Bible Quilt," Georgia, ca. 1886 (plate 40) is a good example of a quilt featuring appliqued pictures and may serve as a source of inspiration for the contemporary quiltmaker.

Harriet Powers, a Negro woman of about forty-nine years of age, exhibited her quilt at the Cotton Fair of 1886 in Athens, Georgia where it captured the imagination of one of the town's residents, Jennie Smith. Miss Smith attempted to buy the quilt, but it was not for sale at any price. Four years later, at her husband's suggestion, Mrs. Powers sought out Miss Smith and agreed to sell the quilt because they needed money.

Using the same prosaic fabrics of which many quilts of the period were composed, this farm woman from the outskirts of Athens, Georgia created this lively, original, and subtly balanced expression of the spiritual influence in her life—her religion. She recorded with familiarity and affection her impressions of highlights of the Old and New Testaments, from the Garden of Eden to the Crucifixion of Christ.

It is most fortunate that Miss Smith recorded Mrs. Powers' verbal descriptions of the quilt's designs. The following is a slightly edited version of the key to the meaning of each section. Miss Smith's comments are included.

1. "represents Adam and Eve in the Garden of Eden, naming the animals and listening to the subtle whisper of the 'serpent beguiling Eve.' It will be noticed that the only animal represented with feet is the only animal that has no feet. The elephant, camel, leviathan, and ostrich appear in this scene."

2. "is a continuation of Paradise, but this time, Eve has 'conceived and born a son' though he seems to have made his appearance in pantaloons, and has made a pet of the fowl. The bird of Paradise in the lower corner is resplendent in green and red calico."

3. "is 'Satan amidst the seven stars,' whatever that may mean, and is not as I first thought a football player. I am sure I have never seen a jauntier devil."

4. "is where Cain 'is killing his brother Abel, and the stream of blood which flew over the earth' is plainly discernible. Abel, being a shepherd, is accompanied by sheep."

5. "Cain here goes into the land of Nod to get him a wife. There are bears, leopards, elks, and a 'kangaroo hog,' but the gem of the scene is an orange colored calico lion in the center who has a white tooth sticking prominently from his lower lip."

6. "is Jacob's dream when 'he lay on the ground' with the angel ascending or descending the ladder."

7. "is the baptism of Christ. The bat-like creature swooping down is 'the Holy

Plate
40

Spirit extending in the likeness of a dove.' "

8. " 'has reference to the Crucifixion.' The globular objects attached to the crosses like balloons by a string represent the darkness over the earth and the moon turning into blood, and is stitched in red and black calico."

9. "This is Judas Iscariot and the thirty pieces of silver. The silver is done in green calico. The large disc at his feet is 'the star that appeared in 1886 for the first time in three hundred years.' "

10. "is the last Supper, but the number of disciples is curtailed by five. They are all robed in white spotted cloth, but Judas is clothed in drab, being a little off-color in character."

11. " 'The next history is the Holy Family; Joseph, the Virgin, and the infant Jesus with the star of Bethlehem over his head. Those are the crosses which he had to bear through his undergoing. Anything for wisement. We can't go back any further than the Bible."

The design of the quilt is made from a

94

combination of pieced work and applique. The applique figures were stitched round by the sewing machine, an unusual way of doing applique at the time. The freedom of this technique is similar to results achieved today by using the zig-zag stitch of the sewing machine. This may partially account for the modernity of the images.

FRIENDSHIP, ALBUM, MARRIAGE, AND PRESENTATION QUILTS

One of the ways of making a quilt was for a group of people to each donate a block. One variation of this practice was the Friendship Quilt which was an expresion of American neighborliness and was part of the tradition of "lending a helping hand" seen in barn and house raisings and corn shucking and quilting bees. Each neighbor gave a block, and all met to set, quilt, and bind the top. The quilts were made for people going west, to help a family get on its feet after a fire, to celebrate a marriage, or honor a minister, teacher, or hero. When the quilt was presented as a token of esteem in a public ceremony, the quilt was called a Presentation Quilt. The blocks were generally decorated with applique, but piecing and embroidery were also used. The choice of design and materials were the responsibility of the individual, but sometimes a theme was decided on such as the Lincoln-Douglas debates, a record of family events, animals in the Bible, or flowers of the area. This latter type of quilt was named an Album Quilt.

The Marriage Quilt, also called the Friendship Medley, was a variety of the Friendship Quilt. Around 1700 an engaged girl would invite her friends to her home to see her wedding presents and help her quilt her Wedding Quilt, the last of her thirteen requisite quilts and the only one that could contain hearts or other symbols of love. Because the superstition grew up that it was bad luck for the engaged girl to work on her own Marriage Quilt, it came to be the custom that the friends of the bride each brought a block, usually appliqued, to her house, then set them together, quilted the top, and presented it to her as a wedding present. In one unusual case in 1877, twenty quilt blocks were designed, initialed, and presented to the bridegroom by twenty of his young lady acquaintances.

Customs varied. In some areas, all the work had to be done by sun down so there could be a big dancing party. Sometimes the blocks were merely presented to the girl, and she and her mother set them together with bright calico strips and quilted the top themselves. As people moved west, the practice spread throughout the country. Around 1900 it died out as small, household gifts were substituted for quilt blocks.

The old tradition of Friendship Quilts is seen again in a quilt made in 1972, "The Hudson River Quilt," (color plate 10). Irene Miller (long active in conservation, author of a book on stitchery, and owner of a textile craft supply shop dedicated to maintaining a living tradition of American crafts) got the idea in 1969 of making an Album or Presentation Quilt about the Hudson River as part of her concern over its decline and destruction.

Source of the Hudson River: Lake Tear of the Clouds Sonna Kates	The Capitol in Albany Ethel Stein	The Alexander Hamilton— Hudson River Day Liner Charlotte Morrill	Olana in Kingston Marjory Payne	The Osborne House in Garrison Leona Dushin
Flowers and Ferns of the Hudson Valley Janet Keppel	Mid-Hudson Bridge at Poughkeepsie Leona Fields	Garrison R.R. Station Marit Kulleseid	Bannerman's Island Carolyn Merritt	Oyster Shells and Blueberry Bushes Carolyn Wilkenson
Storm King Ricci Saunders	West Point Louise Harrienger	The Hudson River Sloop Penny Cohen	Lyndhurst in Tarrytown Corrine Murphy	Croton Point Irene Miller
Stony Point Lighthouse Margaret Harris	Tappan Zee Bridge Elizabeth Downey	Hudson River Museum in Yonkers Michiko Sato	Tappan Oil Tanks in Irvington Gunne Noyes	The Violinist who practices by the River Manine Jones
Ducks of the Hudson River Winifred Lubell	Beart Mt. Bridge and the Highlands Frances Elwyn	Tug Boats Terry Prebble	Sleepy Hollow Country Barbara Bielenberg	Fish of the River Anne Moss
George Washington Bridge and the Little Red Lighthouse Roxa Wright Janet Fiori	Sailboats and the Palisades Dorothy Brightbill	Carl Carmer's Octagonal House in Irvington Catherine McVernon	Manhattan Skyline Wilna Lane	New York Harbour: mouth of the Hudson Constance Cummings

Diagram of "The Hudson River Quilt"

She asked twenty-nine women of her acquaintance (quilters, designers, and people participating in the project) to each donate a block. Each person picked a subject that had meaning to her. The only condition was that the block must represent something still in existence along the Hudson.

The diagram shows the subject each one picked. Charlotte Morril's family had a tradition of traveling every summer on the Alexander Hamilton, a Hudson River Day Liner, and even last summer, after the family had moved to California, their twelve-year-old son returned to take the last trip on the Alexander Hamilton. It was a logical choice for her to applique the ship on the river nosing its ways through the mountains. Marit Kulleseid lives in Garrison, New York, and with embroidery and applique, she stitched the Garrison railroad station where *Hello Dolly* was filmed. She even included the Garrison Art Center (upper right) which overlooks the station. Manine Jones was fascinated by a man who chose to practice his violin between the railroad tracks and the river, so on her block, she caught the bent contours of his body leaning into his music.

When the blocks were finished, the women assembled in the old time manner to set and quilt them.

DESIGNING APPLIQUE

There are several ways of going about designing an applique quilt. The first decision is whether it will be a modern or a traditional quilt. If a traditional quilt is chosen then a design that suits you and/or

the decor the quilt will be used in must be found. This book gives several traditional applique patterns but you might also want to consult *The Standard Book of Quilt Making and Collecting* by Margaret Ickis and Ruby McKim's *One Hundred and One Patchwork Patterns* for others.

A free catalogue of quilt patterns may be obtained by writing to the Stearns and Foster Company, Quilt Department, Cincinnati, Ohio 45215. For thirty-five cents they will send you any pattern listed in the catalogue. Your local library will have a vertical or picture collection which will also contain drawings or photographs of quilts. You can copy these freehand or you can lay a grid drawn on a piece of tracing paper over the picture and copy it square for square onto a similar grid in your notebook. See section on gridding (page 102) for more detailed instructions.

For me though, the most satisfying way of searching for suitable patterns is to look at actual quilts and touch them if possible. Most local museums have a few quilts in their collection, possibly displayed in period rooms. If you wish to look at quilt collections or perhaps buy a few quilts, you would do well to investigate antique shops, county fairs, flea markets, garage sales, and auctions. Start carrying a notebook and whenever you see a quilt pattern you like, make a rough sketch which also indicates its colors.

Our ancestors would collect patterns and keep spare blocks for future reference. Sewing up applique patterns also aids in creating original patterns because the practice helps to develop a feeling for design.

After finding a pattern, the next step is to plan out the top. Make a drawing indicating the size, proportions, and colors of the proposed blocks.

MAKING YOUR OWN DESIGN

Some people work directly with cloth as if they were making a collage out of paper. Jan Eisenman is one such. She couples her responses to everyday, natural subjects to her work with different fabrics. For each applique, she cuts out shapes then pins them in place. Each work is three layers—top, flannel interlining, and backing. In the past she used the sewing machine almost exclusively either to sew close to the edges leaving them raw or to turn under the pieces and stitch a narrow line near the edge. Lately she has gotten back to blind hemming the pieces in place because she likes the way they look, besides which, hand sewing makes the work portable thus freeing her from the fixed position of the sewing machine. The padded figure of the "Woodcock" (plate 41) is made in this way. It is a wall hanging, but the same design could be adapted for making the blocks of a quilt.

"Birds in a Tree" (plate 42) was also made by direct cutting. The tree was stitched down on a linen square with the straight stitch of the sewing machine. Some of the branches and the knots were built up later. The lines of the bark were drawn with the sewing machine. The birds were embroidered.

The way of working I prefer entails first making a freehand drawing on a piece of paper the size of the finished

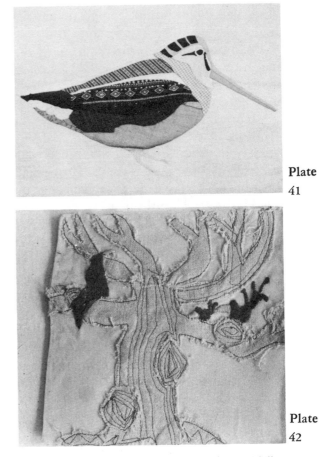

Plate 41

Plate 42

piece. Simple open shapes such as "The Pig" (plate 43) or "The Pick-Up Truck" (plate 44) are easily made by this method. The shapes are then cut out of paper and tried out on a number of fabrics until the cloth that seems right for the subject is found. The shapes are cut out of cloth and pinned on the block. Next they are stitched down with a wide zigzag stitch and then stitched around a second time with a narrower zig-zag stitch with a shorter stitch length. This gives an edge that will withstand washing.

This same technique was used in making "Contact Sheet One—One Cloud, Two Clouds, Three Clouds" (plate 45, color

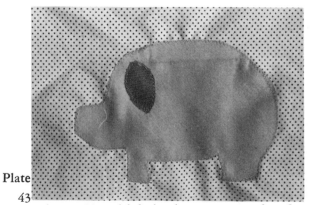

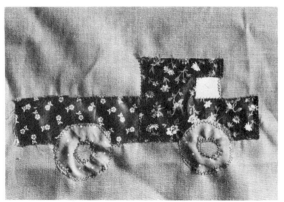

Plate 43

Plate 44

plate 19) which is the passage of a day looking west over the Hudson River. After sewing the pieces down with a zig-zag stitch, they were quilted on the sewing machine. A basting stitch was used for the quilting which follows the outside edges of the zig-zag stitch. The side edges were bound in black and sewn together by hand. The top and bottom strips were then added. "Contact Sheet One . . ." is a study for a twenty block wall quilt.

If you don't feel you have any original drawing ability, you can base your applique work on a design from an outside source. If you have a specific period in mind, library books on the history of interior design, textiles, etc. will be of great help. The illustrations will give you specific patterns to copy or adapt. Books on folk art frequently have striking designs that work well in applique.

Children's coloring books, especially the new ones which are based on drawings by artists of various historical periods (Medieval, Aztec, Egyptian, etc.), give clear outlines and attractive, yet simple designs that can be easily transferred to cloth. Illustrations from a favorite

Plate 45

99

book might be used to make a quilt for a child.

Children's art can be easily translated into applique by any of the methods mentioned earlier, furthermore, a quilt based on your child's artwork makes a nice keepsake for yourself or a lovely gift for a relative. The appliqued picture could be centered and framed with a series of borders. In the past, husbands

Plate 46

Plate 47

Plate 48

100

would sometimes draft a pattern or make a drawing that the wife would then cut and sew.

Start keeping a file of pictures you like from magazines, greeting cards, advertisements, fabrics, or reproductions of fine art. These can be the basis for future designs and will keep you constantly aware of the many possibilities for applique.

Never hesitate to experiment and alter found designs. Any change or alteration of a design makes the work more uniquely yours. Just by looking at the world around you, you will find inspiration for many new and varied applique designs.

REVERSE APPLIQUE

Indian women in Central America embroider the appliqued blocks on their blouses in a special way called "reverse applique." This method creates designs by cutting through layers of cloth. Each blouse design or "mola" is started with five thicknesses of fabric. Each layer is a different, brilliant color. A popular color selection for the layers of a mola would be (going from top to bottom) red, green, blue, orange, and black. The overall shape (such as an outline of a crocodile) is cut out of the top layer, and the edges are sewn under; details such as scales, feet, and legs are made by cutting through to other layers. Regular applique and embroidery stitches are used sparingly to accent these designs.

The Central American Indian women derive their designs from their folk heritage, dealing as it does with animals and geometric shapes, but they are also just

as likely to copy their designs from nature or from tin can labels (and since they cannot read, they include the letters of the alphabet in these "tin can" designs with complete disregard for the meaning of the words formed.) See plates 46, 47, and 48 for traditional mola designs.

The technique of reverse applique can be adapted to contemporary quiltmaking as a way on constructing blocks.

DESIGNING AND MAKING REVERSE APPLIQUE

1. The Indian women did their patterns freehand, but it is simpler in the beginning if a design is planned in advance. Simple shapes are the easiest to manage. It is important to plan for color because the layers of cloth must be in the proper positions in order to provide easy access to the appropriate color.

One way of getting the feel of reverse applique is to make a scratch board. Colored areas of crayon are laid down thickly on a piece of paper or cardboard. The whole sheet is covered with a heavy layer of black crayon. Designs are made by scratching through the black area with a sharp instrument such as a yarn needle, nut pick, or fork and revealing the colored area underneath. Designs in this medium are best made with lines. This would also be the way traditional mola designs are built up.

2. After the number and arrangement of colors has been decided on, baste the fabrics together around the edge and diagonally across so as to hold them securely. In the beginning it is easier to

work with only two or three layers (fig. 3-16a).

3. Trace the outline of the principal shape on the cloth with light pencil or tailor's chalk. To reveal the first color under the top layer, cut through the top layer in the desired shape using sharp pointed scissors (fig. 3-16b).

4. Clip the edges of the fabric. Turn under one eighth of an inch. Blind hem to the next layer using matching thread so that the stitches will be invisible (fig. 3-16c).

5. Continue as above, cutting out layers to reveal the underneath layer until the design is complete. Small appliques or embroidery stitches may be added to complete the work. (fig. 3-16d)

6. The blocks are set together and quilted.

PAINTED QUILTS

With the invention of acrylic (plastic) paint, it has become possible to paint your quilt designs. You might choose a traditional patchwork pattern, but instead of piecing the blocks, the geometric units may be painted on. Drawings that would have ordinarily have become the bases for applique patterns can be drawn instead directly on the cloth and then colored. Folk patterns can also be painted on the cloth (plate 49). Designs may be stenciled or potato prints stamped on the top and then quilted. A child can make his own quilt by painting a picture on a piece of cloth big enough to cover his bed. His mother or teacher would then quilt it for him. Quilted vests and jackets may also be made with this method.

STEPS IN PAINTING A QUILT

1. You will need to buy either a sheet the correct size for the finished quilt, or if you are making blocks, estimate the yardage and buy enough muslin or broadcloth. White cloth is the logical choice for most designs, but any color fabric will do.

You might first want to practice this technique by making a pillow from a small piece of cloth you have already.

Acrylic paint sold in tubes and jars in the right colors is required. It is sold at all art supply stores.

2. Unless you are working directly on the cloth, make a sketch to scale indicating color. To transfer the design, place a grid over the drawing using a straight edge and right angle. Draw a proportionate grid on the sheet in pencil. Transfer the content of each square of the drawing to the corresponding square on the sheet.

3. Mix the acrylic paint with water or medium to a consistency that is thin enough to be absorbed by the cloth but not thin enough to run or lose its color. Experiment on a scrap of cloth until the right consistency is reached.

Pin the sheet to the wall or lay it on the floor. Use a brush and fill in the outlines following your diagram.

If you are not using colors straight from the jar or tube, it will be necessary to have a means of covering and storing the paint. Washed, empty orange juice, yogurt, and cottage cheese containers covered with plastic work well.

4. When the quilt top is dry, it may be quilted. A sheet the same size as the top is bought for the backing. Cotton or dacron sheet batting is laid on top of the backing. The painted top is placed on top and completes the sandwich. Baste or pin the three layers together. Stitch the quilt on the sewing machine. The stitching should follow the outline of the shapes. The quilt is then bound.

Plate 50

Plate 50 Cot quilt; 1972; the designs were painted with acrylic paint. The painted blocks were pieced with calico ones. This quilt was made by the author.

Plate 49

Plate 49 Plumed Serpent design, painted on white cotton with brown acrylic paint; the design was quilted and made into a pillow.

103

QUILTING

"A quilt is not a quilt until it is quilted" says one folk adage. This chapter is about "quilting," or in other words, how to join the three layers of the quilt (top, fill, and backing) by hand or on the sewing machine.

THE FILL OR FILLING

A quilt is a sandwich, and between the top and the bottom layers is what is called the fill or filling in America or the padding in England. The primary purpose of the fill is to provide warmth just as the main function of the quilting stitches is to hold the fill in place. Its secondary function is to give shape to the spaces between the quilting stitches thus throwing the pattern into relief. To serve the first purpose, the fill should be able to reserve heat, and to serve the second, it should be springy and resilient.

Wool was at first used in the West because it was readily available. It seems to have been used into the late eighteenth century in America and well into the nineteenth century in England, however, the following quotation found in a *Compendyous Regyment or a Dietary of Helth* by Andrew Boorde, 1542, gives this advice: "Let your nightcap be of scarlet, and this, I do advertise you, to cause to be made a good thick quilt of cotton, or else of pure flocks or of clean wool, and let the covering of it be of white fustian, and lay it on the featherbed that you do lie on; and in your bed lie not too hot nor too cold, but in temperance." The above quotation makes it clear that by the middle of the sixteenth century raw cotton was considered as a possible alternative to wool for filling quilts.

Before the American Revolution, all materials for quilting including wadding were imported from England. Although cotton was cultivated in Virginia as early as 1621, it was not a staple crop until about 1760; after that the local plantations supplied the fill for American quilts. Florence Peto states that the earliest surviving quilts in America (circa 1750-70) are padded with softest wool. Ruth Finley writes that "not infrequently quilts were filled with fleece, out of necessity rather than choice." Because the fleece was inadequately washed, it retained

much oil and "gave forth a disagreeable odour" in heat or damp atmosphere. Although there is a contradiction in the statements, they are both probably true in fact. Some of the immigrants had learned how to thoroughly wash wool from their mothers or in their home countries, but others, including the Dutch who quilted cotton and had been trading in the East, had never used wool before and therefore did not know how to scour it properly. Eli Whitney perfected his cotton gin in 1793, and ginned cotton became plentiful during the following ten to twenty years. In America this marks the beginning of the widespread use of cotton as the fill. In times of scarcity though, "waste not, want not" became the governing principle for selecting the fill, and an old blanket, an old quilt, newspapers, old clothes, or corn husks were substituted for materials especially designed for filling a quilt.

Today we can go to the bedding department of the department store or to a needlework or crafts supply store and buy a roll of batting in the correct size. It comes in cotton and dacron in three sizes—crib, standard bed, and extra large bed. Although dacron costs more, many people prefer it because they say it retains its shape better and is easier to handle. If an extra thick quilt is desired, two bats should be bought, and the second one is laid on the first. Scraps of batting left over from making a large quilt may be laid in overlapping strips or pieces to make a crib quilt or a bed cover.

Other materials other than the ones already mentioned may also be used for the fill. Quilters are experimenting today with sheets of polyurethane foam which can be bought in quilt sized bats designed as mattress covers. Its advantage is supposed to lie in the material's ability to retain its body with repeated washings. The new acrylic blankets are inexpensive, washable, easy to manipulate, and make a good filling for a quilt. Feathers and down are used to fill comforters.

THE BACKING

The backing is the bottom most layer of the quilt. It is usually made from muslin or other firm, inexpensive cloth. It may be any color (some backs are even pieced from remnants), but the most popular color has always been white. Because of its durability, natural, undyed homespun was used for backing a long time after machine-made cloth was used for tops. The lengths of cloth that make the backing are sewn together on the sewing machine until the desired width is reached. The bedding department of the department store sells extra wide muslin sheeting designed to be used as a quilt back. It comes in 72-inch and 90-inch widths. This muslin is sometimes packaged in standard sizes. Buying bed sheets, especially seconds, is a good way of getting an inexpensive, colored backing.

THE QUILTING FRAME

Traditionally, the quilt top, filling, and back are put into a homemade stretcher called a quilting frame so that they may be held taut while the layers are being quilted together. If you are going to quilt

with the sewing machine, sew your quilt in your lap, or send it out to be quilted, this section may be disregarded until you decide to try your hand at the craft of quilting.

The stretcher is made from four strips of wood, ordinarily one inch thick, two to four inches wide and four feet long. A frame is only fully extended at American quilting bees where women would work along the sides. Normally the side pieces which are adjustable are shortened to about four feet in length. The four corners of the frame are fastened together with wooden pegs thrust through holes pierced through the ends of the strips of wood. A series of holes is necessary to allow the width of the frame to be adjusted (fig. 4-1). The frame corners are today more commonly fastened with metal "C" clamps purchased in any hardware store (fig. 4-2). Either an inch wide strip of heavy cloth is tacked along the edges of the frame or heavy muslin is wrapped around the end bars and securely tacked or sewn. The quilt is attached to the cloth. Historically, the frame was supported on four quilting chairs which are now known by antique dealers as "arrow-backs," "Windsors," "fan-backs," "Hitchcocks," and "low ladder backs." All these are chairs which have knobs or projections above the last slat of the backrest on which the frame can be supported. Today such a frame would be balanced on saw horses or, as one young woman in Brooklyn, New York is currently doing, suspended by ropes from the ceiling and raised and lowered with pulleys.

In the past, women worked on their

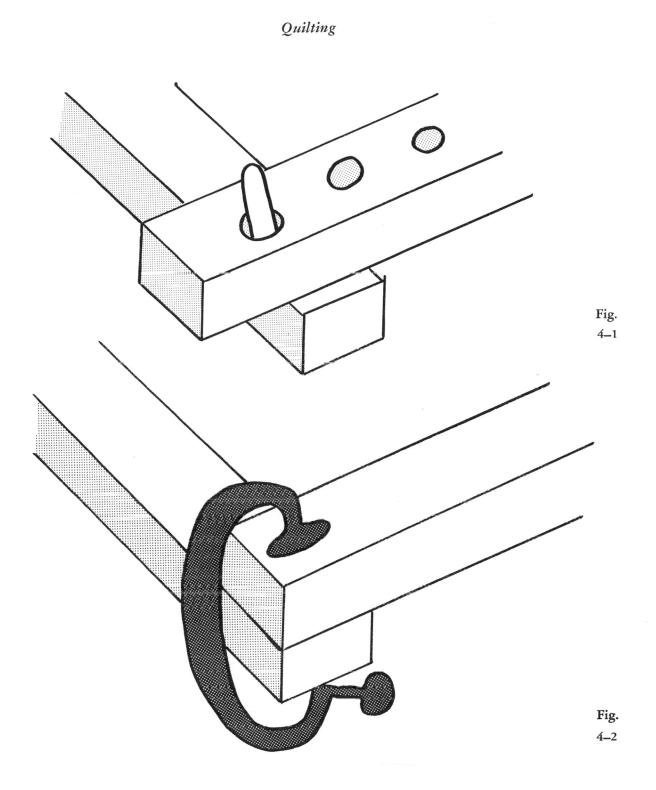

Fig.
4–1

Fig.
4–2

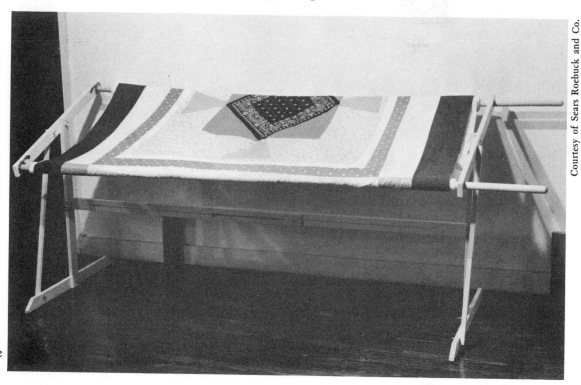

Courtesy of Sears Roebuck and Co.

Plate
51

quilts in the parlor, proud to display their handiwork. The biggest obstacle to the use of the traditional quilting frame today is that the frame should be left in place until the quilt is finished. Most women today do not want a quilting frame permanently set up in the middle of the living room, therefore, a room that is not used too much is usually desired. If the quilt frame must be dismantled, remove the side bars and roll up the quilt on the long bars. It may now be leaned against a wall or put in a closet.

Fixed and tilt-top quilting frames (plate 51) are available from needlework shops and large mail order companies such as Sears Roebuck. These have ratchets which enable the quilt to be wound without dismantling the frame.

Twenty-two-inch quilting hoops are also commercially available. The hoop is attached with an adjustable arm to a stand.

PUTTING IN—ASSEMBLING THE QUILT IN THE FRAME

In the past when one neighbor would say to another, "I put in yesterday," it meant that she had put the quilt (top, fill, and backing) in the frame. There are two methods of doing this. The first is the traditional method, and the second which I call basting is also used when preparing the quilt for the sewing machine or for lap quilting as well as for the quilting frame.

The traditional way of "putting in" the

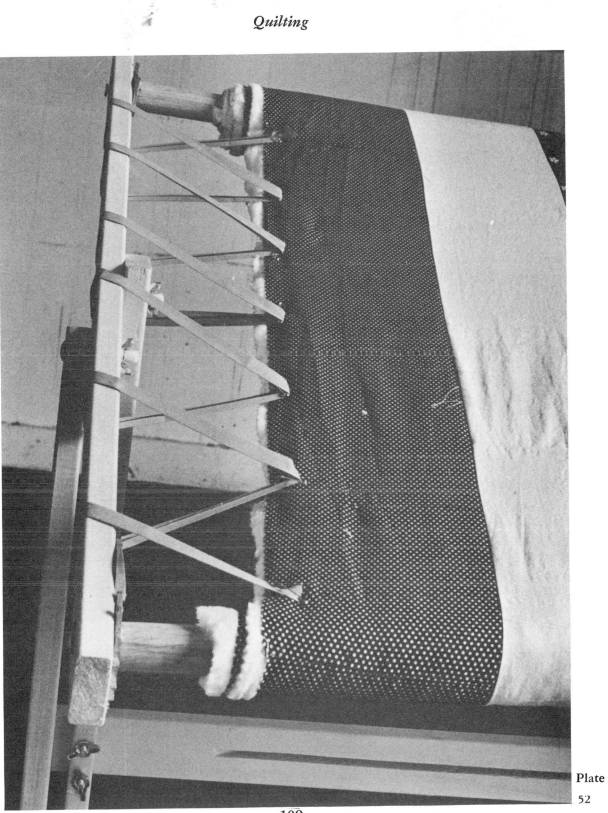

Plate
52

quilt is to open the frame to its fullest width. This should be the width of the quilt plus twelve inches. The frame is placed on the floor with the corners secured. The backing is pulled between the two long bars and securely sewn to the cloth wrapped around them. The bat is then carefully unrolled on top of the backing and spread to the edges. The quilt top is placed on top of the bat. It must be spread gently and evenly because this is the point where imperfections in sewing and piecing will show up. These, however, can be adjusted by proper quilting. The edges of the top are basted to the bat and the backing. Over half of the quilt is then rolled up on one bar and the frame is clamped together at its narrower width.

Button thread or carpet thread is run in zig-zags through the edge of the quilt and the frame. Bias tape may be substituted for button thread. If you use bias tape, you will need a package of it and approximately fifteen medium sized safety pins. The tape is first pinned (through all three layers) to the quilt with safety pins, then it is passed around the frame, returned to the quilt, and pinned in place. The process is continued until the edge of the quilt is held taut to the side of the frame. Cut the tape. Repeat on the other side (plate 52).

BASTING

Basting is an alternative way of preparing the quilt for all types of quilting. The back is laid on a large flat surface such as the floor. The batting is rolled out on top of it so that there are no lumps or

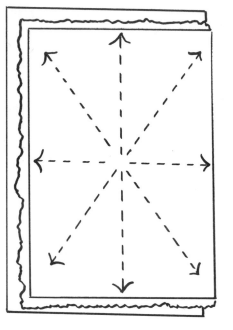

Fig. 4–3

thin places. The batting is fastened to the back with long basting stitches. Start in the center of the quilt and sew till you have the diagonal lines shown in figure 4-3. Iron the quilt top removing all wrinkles and creases. The top is now laid in place over the fill and backing. Be sure the edges match up with the bottom layers on all sides. The three layers are basted together in the same manner as the first two were, that is with diagonal lines radiating out from the center. The quilt is now ready to be put into the frame or be quilted on the sewing machine.

The quilt is put into the frame by securely sewing one end of the quilt to the strip of cloth tacked to the long bar of the quilting frame. Most of the quilt is rolled up on this bar. The opposite end of the quilt is sewn to the cloth strip on the other long bar. The quilting frame is clamped together with the quilt being held taut between the two bars. The sides of the quilt are held in place by making a zig-zag stitch with carpet thread between the edge of the quilt and the quilting frame.

MARKING

Before quilting, the design must be marked on the quilt. This may be done before or after the quilt is put into the frame. But even if you mark after you have "put in" the quilt, a grid which will enable the designs to be centered is usually laid down beforehand. There are several methods of marking and you will have to decide which one suits you before the quilt is put into the frame.

In some areas of America and England, marking the quilt tops was a profession. Special quilts such as Wedding Quilts which were going to receive more elaborate quilting than usual were sent out to be marked. Also, women who did not have the time or drafting ability sent out their quilts to be marked. In England blue pencil markings were used so that the lines would show up clearly and so that they could be easily followed by someone not familiar with the pattern. The disadvantage was that the lines could be clearly seen until the quilt was washed for the first time. Interestingly enough, Mavis Fitzrandolph says that, "Some old ladies in the North cherish quilts by George Gardiner (a famous quilter and marker) and deliberately keep them unwashed 'so that the marks will show'!"

Until recently in America, quilting patterns were bought stamped on paper.

These were traced on the material with a spur rowel or rowelled dressmaking wheel and dressmaker's tracing paper. You can make your own perforated patterns by enlarging and transferring any of the quilting patterns given onto heavy paper or special stencil paper which may be purchased at art supply stores. Go over the pattern with a tracing wheel perforating it. Dust charcoal or stamping powder through the holes. The powder may be blown off when the quilting is done.

Diagonal lines in sets of two or three make a pattern called "The Double and Triple Diagonals" (fig. 4-4). When the diagonal lines are crossed they form diamonds. Traditionally, straight lines were marked by chalking a cord (rubbing chalk on a cord). It was held firmly at one end. A second person pulled the string tight and then snapped it. The flying string left a line. Traditionally, a bride could snap her Wedding Quilt but could not quilt it. Today most people would prefer using a ruler to make a straight line.

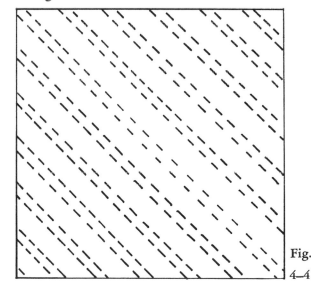

Fig. 4-4

Plate
53

TEMPLATES

"Scratching" is another way of marking a top. A rowel, a needle, or a special tool made by inserting a needle into a cork (eye end out) are used to make a mark on the cloth. The needle is not held upright but at a sharp angle and is pressed firmly, leaving a mark like a crease. Only a small area may be marked by this method at a time because the line disappears.

Of course with pencil or tailor's chalk, many quilters prefer to draw their patterns freehand. The freedom of a great number of American quilts suggest that this was a common approach in the United States. (plate 53)

More common in England than in America, templates (fig. 4-5) (shapes made of paper, cardboard, wood, or tin) are used as a pattern for maintaining the regular outlines of the quilting patterns. Templates may be drafted by the quiltmaker or members of the family. They were frequently passed down through the generations. The template shape is outlined on the top. Any fill (elaborate inner stitches) is put in freehand.

A variation on the template is the use of household objects such as glasses, saucers, cups, plates, pans, and coins for drawing patterns on the top. Mavis Fitzrandolph quotes an old English quilter,

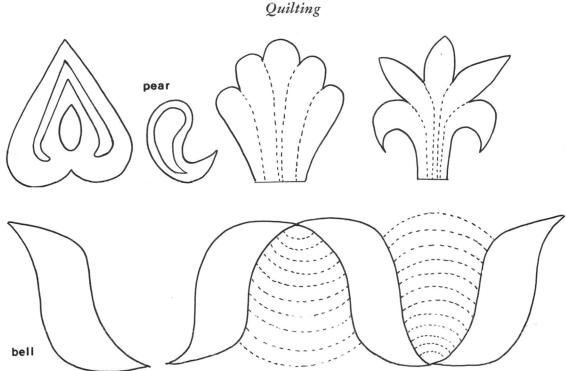

pear

bell

Fig.
4–5

"The fun we were having making designs, many a time we were putting a pan upside down so as to have a circle even." The most popular design using a household object was called "Wine-Glass" (fig. 4-6) and consisted of overlapping circles. The design was drafted, strangely enough, with the aid of a wineglass. The pattern was used for an overall design on small quilts and as a border on large ones where it was called "Tea Cup" because a tea cup was used to draft it. The concentric semicircles used to quilt "The Cactus Rose" (plate 20) quilt are called "Plate" because a plate was used to draw them.

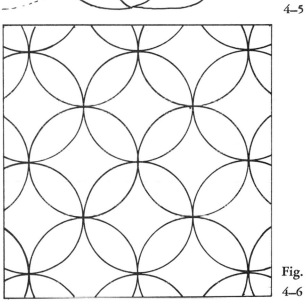

Fig.
4–6

QUILTING PATTERNS

Strictly, quilting is a form of practical sewing in which short running stitches are used to join the three layers of the quilt. Today we have a tendency to think of the top as the work of art and ignore the importance of the quilting. Quilting, however, throws the applique or patchwork pattern into relief. It is the quilting stitches which subtly transform the surface of the quilt into a play of light and shadow. Rose Wilder Long describes the important function of the stitches:

> You may quilt in any color but you are not working with color; you are working with light. To contrast with shadows, the light must lie on a smooth surface. So the pattern is the untouched surface of the cloth. It stands out in bas-relief because the light on it is unbroken. The quilting makes the background of tiny hills of cloth that break up the light with their shadows.

Plate 54

The two simplest methods of quilting were: a) to quilt straight lines and b) to outline patchwork or applique patterns with quilting stitches. If the worked squares had been set with plain squares, the patchwork or applique patterns were repeated in quilting stitches on the plain block. The back of the modern "Coarse Woven Patch" quilt (plate 54) shows this practice.

But the women always regarded quilting as a separate art, and whenever possible, they escaped from simply utilitarian methods. They could not resist adding little pictures such as the griffin (plate 55) from a 1703 English coverlet.

Plain quilts or all-white quilts were made from the eleventh century. These were quilts in which quilting stitches were the sole means of decoration. These quilts reached their highest development in the sixteenth and seventeenth centuries. The all-white quilt was popular in America from the late eighteenth to the early nineteenth century. Pieces were made by women of the higher social classes because they were the only ones that had the time to make the endless small stitches necessary for forming the designs. The designs were padded to throw them into greater relief. These quilts represented the epitome of quilting in America. The decline of this type of quilt corresponded with the invention of the Jacquard loom in about 1809. It was possible to obtain similar effects with less effort using that machine, and there de-

114

Plate
55

veloped the Marseilles spread which was made on the Jacquard loom and which had a long period of popularity. The custom of dressing beds in white continued throughout the nineteenth century. Women too poor to afford new spreads would turn over their old patchwork quilts and display them on their beds with the white side up showing the quilting pattern. Thus for decorative purposes, these women had two quilts for the price of one.

In America, quilting was basically a two-step process. First the patchwork or applique pattern was outlined with thin concentric lines of stitching until the

Fig. 4–7

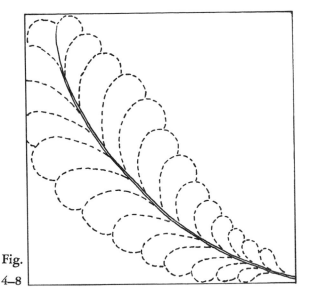

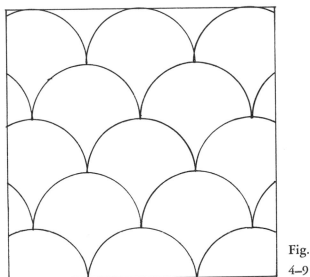

Fig. 4–8

Fig. 4–9

edges of the blocks were reached. Second, the plain blocks interspersed between the pieced or appliqued blocks were quilted with large, unitary patterns such as elaborate wreaths (fig. 4-7). Tradition dictated which particular quilting patterns would be used with particular patchwork or applique patterns. "Feathers" (fig. 4-8) were often quilted to fill the plain white border which was used to display the quilting. An outlined cardboard pattern was used to make a popular allover quilting design called "Clam Shell" (fig. 4-9). This design resembles overlapping fish scales. Occasionally, an open space was left in the center of the quilt to allow space for a quilted picture such as a ship in full sail, the American eagle, or a basket of fruit spilling grapes. However, in America, largely because of the pressures of necessity, quilting often remained utilitarian.

In England quilting was a profession and an art. Most quilters worked out their patterns as they went along. Mavis Fitzrandolph quotes an old Welshwoman as saying, "It is a lovely work, and very interesting to see your patterns form under your hand." The quilting was designed separately from the pattern of the top. They used templates for standard patterns, but the names of the pattern units suggest they were copied from commonplace objects: "plait," "chain," "hour glass," "pair of scissors," "bellows," "plate," "basin," "flat iron," "hammock," "bell," "goose wing," "coxcomb," "fan," "shell," "dogs' teeth," "worm," "sheff of corn." One woman in Northumberland, wanting something to fill a space on a quilt, made a template from a clothes brush and used this twice, one shape across another. Another woman designed a pattern unit from the embossed leather binding of the family Bible. She made a simplified drawing, enlarged it, and then made a template.

How does a quilter who does not use perforated patterns and mark out the quilt beforehand design a quilt? Mavis

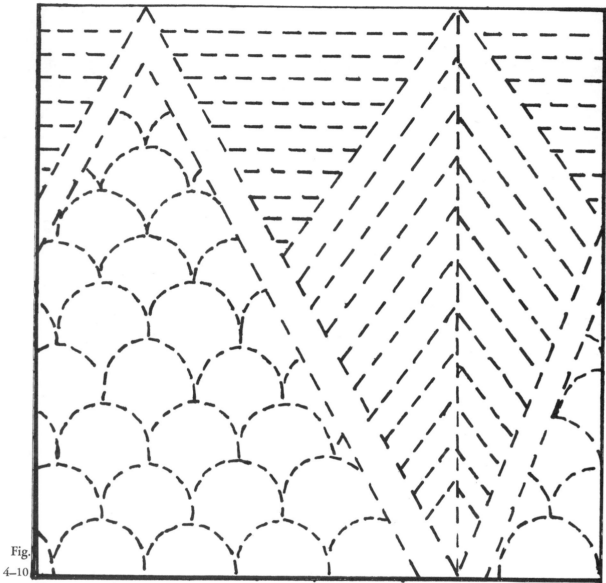

Fig.
4–10

Fig. 4–10 "Cloud Quilting"

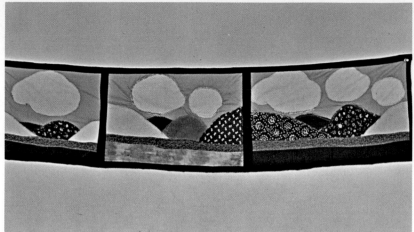

19

19 Contact Sheet—One Cloud, Two Clouds, Three Clouds, 1972, 12″ x 47″, made by Ann-Sargent Wooster
20 Pink Crosses, 1971-72, made by Michiko Sato
21 Brown and Black, 1971-72, made by Michiko Sato

20

21

22

22 Emir's Palace, silk, batiste cotton batiks, and mirrors, made by Jodi Robbin

23 Kimono Quilt, 1971-72, made by Michiko Sato

24 Maple Leaf Photo Quilt, 1972, photographic linen and cotton, made by Amy Stromsten

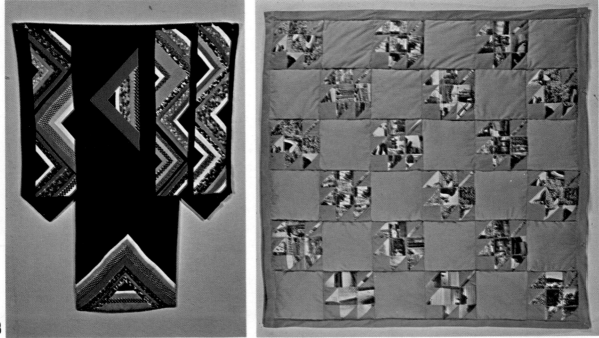

23   24

Fig.
4–11

Fig. 4–11 "Sea Waves"

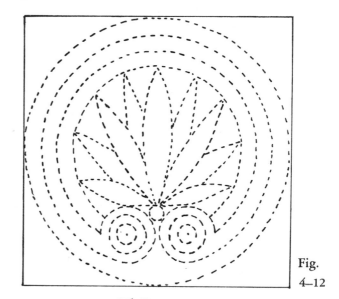

Fig.
4–12

Fig. 4–12 "Water Lily"

Fitzrandolph quotes the following stories which are probably equally true for the individual quilter in America.

> Miss Emiah Jones of Carmarthenshire, a notable Welsh quilter, once said that her mother was "wonderful at giving her a mind-picture of the design she wanted us to do"; father then drew it in chalk on the kitchen flagstones, at her direction.

> Another Welshwoman told how she woke in the night with the plan for her next quilt in her mind, lighted a candle and sketched it on the wallpaper so that she would not forget it.

Few British quilters kept books of patterns, but most could reproduce any pattern they ever made. English quilting represents a living tradition with the patterns constantly changing. This attitude should be the watchword of all your creative work. Never be merely a copyist. Feel free to alter patterns to make them more truly yours.

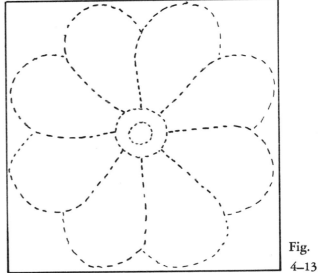

Fig.
4–13

Fig. 4–13 "Daisy"

119

Plate
56

Plate 56 The quilting stitch—the needle is pushed vertically downward.

Plate
57

Plate 57 The quilting stitch—with one hand in position under the quilting frame, the needle is pushed back up to complete the stitch.

THE QUILTING STITCH

By definition quilting means making fairly small running stitches through three layers of material. This is fairly easy to do if the object being quilted is in your lap; the material may be bunched up and two hands used. The needle takes three or four stitches in a line, and the thread is pulled through. To understand quilting, it is a good idea to make a small practice piece such as a cushion cover. Once the quilt is in the frame, you must learn a new method of sewing. The most accurate and most time consuming method is the two step, up and down stitch. With one hand, the needle is pushed vertically downward (plate 56) from the top, and with the other hand in position under the frame, the needle is pushed back up to complete the stitch (plate 57).

In the traditional method of quilting, the needle is held at an acute angle, the quilter holds her left hand under the work, and as one craftswoman describes it, she senses where the needle will come through and helps it back. Her right thumb is extended at every stitch to press the material down slightly just ahead of where the needle will come up. Doing this, your left thumb will get very sore unless you tape it, use a thimble, or use your fingernail. At quilting bees, small children were stationed under the frame and they would help push the needles back up.

NEEDLE AND THREAD

To quilt use a short, sharp needle and about eighteen inches of 40-60 thread in a color that matches the design. A special thread coated with silicone to help it slide easily through thick fabrics is now being marketed for quilting.

Some quilters thread several needles at a time and leave them stuck in the side of the quilt ready for use. When you are ready to use a new needle and thread, a knot is made at the end of the thread. In order not to leave any rough spots on the quilt, the knot must be pulled into the batting.

QUILTING BEES

In America, work parties were called bees. Quilting bees were one of the most popular ways for women to get together socially. The bee pictured in plate 58 is taking place in the winter, but this was unusual because few homes had a warm space big enough to set up an eight foot quilting frame. Usually the winter was spent making tops. Because it took anywhere from two weeks to two months to quilt a quilt alone, when the weather warmed, a group of neighbors would gather at one house and set up two or three quilting frames on the porch or under the shade of the trees. The day was spent quilting, and in the evening, the men folk came over for a dance which

Plate
58

not infrequently involved romance for as the song says, "It was from Aunt Dinah's quilting party I was seeing Nellie home."

One pair of sisters in the nineteenth century were so finicky about their quilting that after having the neighbors over for the sociability of the quilting bee, they would rip out the stitches and requilt the quilt with their own beautiful patterns and precise stitches.

TYING A QUILT

A tied quilt is the simplest form of quilting. The top is merely joined to the fill and backing by means of yarn or thread pulled through and back then knotted. This is done at regular intervals.

The tufts are frequently left as decoration. Tying is used when time is at a premium or when no fill is used so that elaborate quilting is not warranted or when the top is too thick to permit easy passage of the needle.

QUILTING ON THE SEWING MACHINE

1. Be sure that all three layers of the quilt are securely basted together. Try to work on a large table which will support the weight of the quilt.
2. Loosen the tension, raise the presser foot, and set the stitch length to six or eight. Use 40-60 thread, the same color as the area to be quilted.

3. If you are quilting in diagonals (fig. 4-14), fold the quilt in half diagonally and iron the crease. Fold the quilt in the opposite direction and again iron the crease. Following the arrows, sew the two center diagonals. Mark the rest of the diagonals with a yardstick. Following the arrows, sew the rest of the diagonals alternating directions.

4. Patchwork and applique shapes are normally outlined. Stitching is made one quarter of an inch from the seam. If a hand quilted effect is desired, lift the needle at every seam junction leaving a loop of thread. The threads are cut and knotted later.

5. Since no more than four square inches of the quilt should be left unquilted, the remaining areas are filled in with concentric lines, one inch apart, outlining the patchwork or appliqued shape. These lines would be drawn on the top with a ruler or a straightedge.

To make borders, I like to divide the alloted area into squares with a ruler and then divide those squares diagonally in half thus making two triangles. I then quilt a smaller triangle in the center of each of the bigger triangles (fig. 4-15).

6. Fancy quilt patterns may be made by removing the presser foot or, in newer

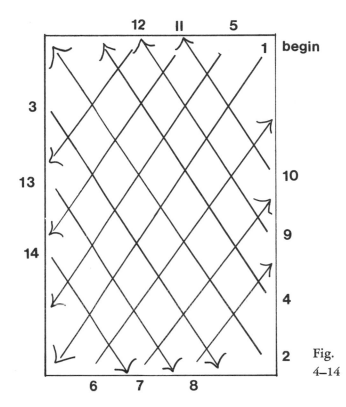

Fig. 4–14

machines, by setting the pressure dial to darning (zero). A large embroidery hoop is then placed on the quilt. With the pressure loosened, the design may be followed freely. Because the machine can no longer regulate its pressure, care must be taken that the stitches are of uniform tightness and length.

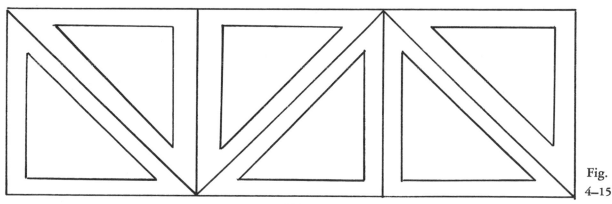

Fig. 4–15

PADDING

Quilting designs that have raised portions are padded. Stems and thin scrolls are made by inserting thick string under the top while it is being quilted. Broad areas are thrust into relief by inserting extra batting after the pattern is quilted. This is accomplished by making a small hole in the back of the quilt and using a yarn needle, crochet hook, or other pointed implement to push wadding through the hole until the design is stuffed full. Care must be taken that the padding is smooth and even. I have discovered that dacron stuffing makes a better padding material than cotton. (fig. 4-16)

The "Garden of Eden" quilt (plate 59) was made on the sewing machine. It is a variation of the traditional all-white

Plate 59

Plate 60

Plate 60 Detail of the "Garden of Eden" quilt

quilt and relies on the play of light on the surface to reveal the contours of the forms. The animals were made into a bas-relief by filling them very full with dacron stuffing.

The pearl stitch is a small bead-like stitch which was used in conjunction with padding to give greater emphasis to the quilting stitches. The pearl stitches were each taken over three threads of ninety-threads-to-the-inch fabric. Make a single stitch but before drawing it tight, bring up the thread and pass it through the loop. The stitch is then drawn tight. The "pearl" is formed by the extra thread lying on top of the first stitch.

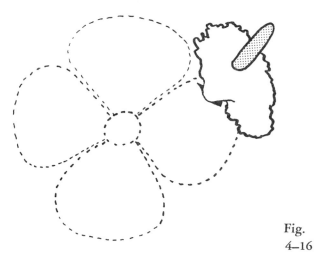

Fig. 4–16

TRAPUNTO OR ITALIAN QUILTING

Trapunto is a way of making a high-relief design. Through two or more layers, the design is outlined with a double row of running stitches. Rug yarn or orlon bulky yarn is drawn between the double lines of quilting throwing the design into strong relief (fig. 4-17a). Bring the needle out the back at angles or sharp curves in the design. Insert the needle again leaving a small loop. This will prevent the padding from shrinking when the quilt is washed (fig. 4-17b).

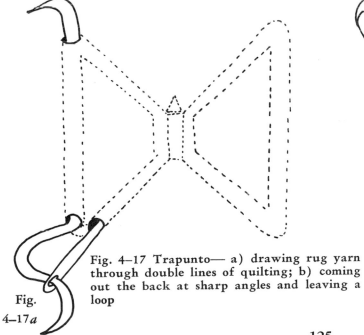

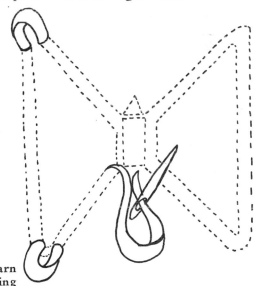

Fig. 4-17 Trapunto— a) drawing rug yarn through double lines of quilting; b) coming out the back at sharp angles and leaving a loop

Fig. 4–17*a*

Fig. 4–17*b*

BINDING

The raw edges of the completed quilt must be finished or bound. This is done in several ways. A narrow edge of backing can be turned over on the top and hemmed down. The edges of the back and top can be turned in and run together by hand or on the sewing machine. A separate strip of cloth can be stitched around the quilt on the sewing machine (fig. 4-18a). Commercial hem facing or bias tape is now also used. It is turned back over the edge and blind hemmed in place (fig. 4-18b). This, in my opinion, is the best method because binding wears out and must be periodically renewed.

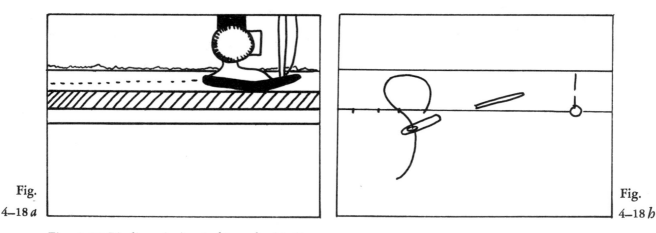

Fig.
4—18 *a*

Fig.
4—18 *b*

Fig. 4—18 Binding— a) stitching the binding strip on the sewing machine; b) turning the binding strip over the edge of the quilt and blind hemming it in place

OTHER USES FOR PATCHWORK, APPLIQUE, AND QUILTING

Patchwork, applique, and quilting have a long tradition of being used for purposes other than the creation of bedcovers. Patchwork was used for fancy mending and flag making. Applique has a long history as a decorative art. Clothes, banners, and ecclesiastical garments have all benefited from its application. Quilting began as a way of padding winter garments, and the Chinese still widely use it as such. Western knights, borrowing the idea from the Saracens, wore quilted shirts to keep their armor from chafing. Some of these quilted shirts were supposed to be so finely made, they could be drawn through a ring. The common soldier who could not afford armor or the horse necessary to support it wore shirts of flax tow quilted in lozenges, squares, or lines between canvas and leather in order to deflect the force of an arrow. In the days before central heating, men wore fancy quilted vests. These were popular from 1550 to 1800. Ladies wore quilted petticoats from 1500 to 1800. When fashion decreed that the overskirts be pulled back to reveal the quilted petticoats, those petticoats were made of silk and ornamented with elaborate quilting, gold thread, and pearls. Samuel Pepys' maid servant, so the story goes, stole his best quilt and, when found, had made it into the then fashionable petticoats. In rural areas in England and America, quilted petticoats were worn for warmth well into the late nineteenth century.

MAKING A PILLOW WITH BORDERS

Nowadays pillows are the first use for patchwork that comes to mind. Phyllis Luberg of New York City's first project after having learned to use a sewing machine was to put borders on some individual blocks she had bought at an antique shop and then fashion those blocks into pillows. Her friends liked the results so well that she and her friend Jane Lyons began making more pillows. They quickly used up the blocks which Phyllis had first bought and which had come from an old lady's collection of patterns. They began looking for unquilted tops and damaged quilts to turn into pillows. This sent them to New Jersey, Pennsylvania, and North Carolina. (In North

Carolina, when asked if they had any old quilts, the people replied, "Kwelts! What do you want with old kwelts?") Some of the results of their searches may be seen in many of the old quilts in this book and the bordered pillows seen in color plates 11 and 13.

If you have any spare blocks or have been making practice blocks and want to adapt them so as to make a pillow, the easiest way to enlarge and enliven the

Plate 61

Plate 61 A pillow made from strips of cloth pieced into a square on the sewing machine, it was surrounded by two borders then machine quilted.

128

patch is to put borders on it until the desired size is reached. (plate 61)

1. First decide what color scheme you want for the borders. It will take one quarter to one third of a yard for each border.

2. Cut or tear the cloth into strips of the desired width. Pin a strip of cloth to the top and bottom of the patch and stitch with a quarter-of-an-inch seam (fig. 5-1a). Press the seams toward the center.

5. You will need material for the cushion backing. The material may either pick up or accent a color or fabric from the cushion top or be of a different color or fabric. Place the cushion top on the backing material and use it as a pattern. Pin the right sides of the top and backing together. Sew around three sides. Leave an opening on one side to allow space for inserting the stuffing.

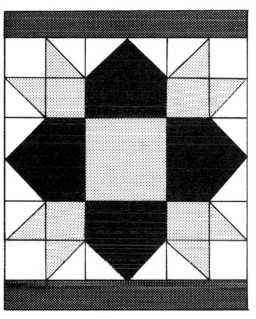

Fig. 5–1*a*

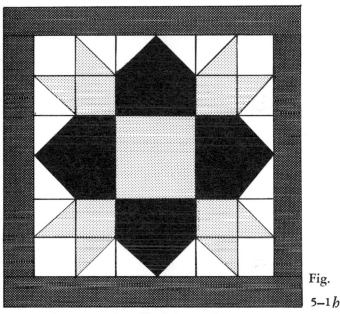

Fig. 5–1*b*

3. Cut two strips of cloth, each the length of the patch plus the top and bottom borders (fig. 5-1b). Stitch the seams.

4. If more borders are wanted, proceed as above, remembering to press the seams toward the center. This technique is similar to the one used to make a "Log Cabin" quilt. If a strip is not long enough, stitch another piece onto it. The extra seam does not matter.

6. Stuff. Shredded foam, kapok, a precut foam rubber shape, or dacron stuffing may all be used. Dacron stuffing gives the smoothest feeling. Turn the edges of the opening in and sew together with tiny stitches.

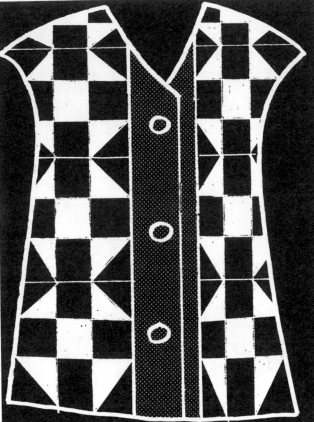

Fig.
5–2

USING PATCHWORK

Anything that can be made from plain cloth can be made from pieced cloth, but simple shapes should be chosen to allow the patterns to be fully displayed.

1. Unless an unquilted top is inherited or purchased, it is best to start by making something small such as a tie, belt, glasses case, or bag. Even on the sewing machine, the piecing takes quite a while. Pick a simple pattern. The basic principle is to piece only as much as is needed in order to cut out the pattern. Remember you are not making yard goods. It is important to cut all the pieces following the grain line and to press the seams toward the center. Strips of plain cloth may be added (see vest, fig. 5-2) to extend the pieced area. The effect achieved will be very similar to that of setting pieced blocks with plain ones when making a quilt top.

2. Iron the patchwork. Place the pattern on the pieced cloth. Pin. Cut out.

3. (If you are quilting the object, see section on quilting small objects at the end of this chapter.) All pieced work should be lined, both to feel more comfortable to the wearer and to protect the seams. Place the cut out shape on a piece of batiste or other lining material and cut out. Baste the two layers together and treat as one piece for the rest of the sewing. Items that are not going to receive much wear, however, such as a tie or a cushion cover do not absolutely need to be lined.

A BELT

Any simple, striped patchwork pattern or "Crazy" work is easily converted into a belt. The belt shown here (plate 62) was made from "Dog's Tooth" triangles in shades of blue and brown.

1. Piece the material to the desired length.

2. Cut a strip of muslin the same size as the finished strip. Lay batting on top of the muslin strip. Trim the batting.

3. Pin or baste the three layers together. Quilt on the sewing machine following the outline of the patchwork pattern. The quilting gives strength and shape to the belt.

4. Bind the quilted strip with bias tape or strips of cloth. Sew two rings or other belt fastenings at the ends of the belt.

Plate
62

Plate
63

A GLASSES CASE

A quilted glasses case is a colorful way of protecting sun glasses or regular glasses, and it makes a good present.

1. Piece an approximately six by eight inch rectangle from a patchwork pattern. Pick one that will look good when divided in half. The one shown here (plate 63) was made from strips of cloth sewn together on the sewing machine.

2. Cut a piece of muslin or other soft material the same size as the pieced rectangle. Spread batting on the muslin backing.

3. Quilt the pieced material, batting, and backing together on the sewing machine following the seams of the piecing. Bind one short side of the rectangle with a contrasting strip of cloth or bias tape. This will be the mouth of the case. Fold the rectangle in half so that the two long sides are touching with the patchwork side out. Pin. Bind the side raw edges together. Bind the bottom.

132

Courtesy of The Grand Hotel

Plate
64

Plate
65

HANDBAGS

A simple shoulder bag is made from two ten- by fifteen-inch rectangles in the "Cotton Reel" pattern (plate 64). The rectangles are joined at what will be the bottom of the bag with a three- by fifteen-inch strip of blue and white polka dotted cotton. The large rectangle formed by sewing these three pieces together is quilted on the sewing machine. Now bind the other fifteen-inch edges with strips of blue and white polka dotted material. Fold up the large rectangle and sew a separating zipper between the top edges.

The side edges are next bound and joined with blue and white polka dotted material. The rings and the quilted strap are sewn on.

Another simple bag is made from several blocks taken from a silk antique "Log Cabin" quilt (plate 65). The pattern is different on each side. Jackie Lewis, who designed the bag, collects her findings (clasp bar and handle) by taking apart old bags she finds at auctions.

Many of the large pattern companies have handbag patterns. These might be used to make bags from pieced or print material which you have quilted.

Plate
66

Plate
67

TIES

Ties are an excellent choice for patchwork. Tie patterns are made by major pattern companies, or a pattern may be drafted by tracing a tie. Choose plain or print cottons for the summer and silks, velveteens, velvets, or wool for the winter. The "Pinwheel" tie (plate 66) was made from pink and dark cottons for a June birthday. For a January birthday, the "Grandmother's Postage Stamp" tie (plate 67) was pieced from green and purple calicoes and blue velveteen. Both ties were pieced on the sewing machine.

CLOTHES

Both regular and floor length wrap-around skirts are good styles for using patchwork material or an old quilt (fig. 5-3). Vests (fig. 5-2) and jackets (plates 70, 71, 72), are other good ways of displaying patchwork cloth or old quilts. If you are using an old quilt or quilted material to make clothes, remember to cut the pattern slightly larger to allow for the extra thickness of the material.

Fig. 5–3

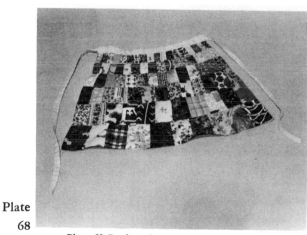

Plate 68

Plate 68 Patchwork apron; courtesy of Liberty Crafts

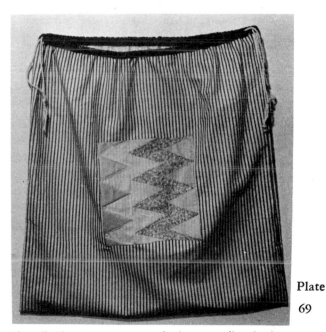

Plate 69

Plate 69 Zig-zag pattern rectangle, it was appliqued onto a blue and white striped ticking draw string bag.

Courtesy of The Grand Hotel

Courtesy of The Grand Hotel

Plate
70

Plate
71

Plate
72

Plate 72 Jacket made from portions of "Necktie," "Grandmothers Flower Garden," and "Hole in the Barn Door" unquilted tops; courtesy of The Grand Hotel

Plate
73

APPLIQUE

Applique began as a way of decorating clothes. Small shapes such as diamonds and flowers were snipped out of cloth and stitched down. It has remained a perennially popular form of ornamentation. There are several ways of using applique to decorate clothes, bags, belts, pillows, etc. They reflect the traditional and modern methods and attitudes of quiltmaking.

1. A shape drawn on a piece of paper can be used for a pattern to cut out the cloth. Remember to add a quarter of an inch seam allowance. The design may be an adaptation of a traditional quilt block such as the neckline decorated with "The Hollyhock Wreath" pattern (fig. 5-4) or it may be a special design such as the whimsical pig which is shown stitched on a pinafore (fig. 5-5). The shapes are pinned in place on an already completed garment, or they are pinned onto the material after it has been cut out but before it is stitched together. The edges are notched, turned under, and blind hemmed into place.

138

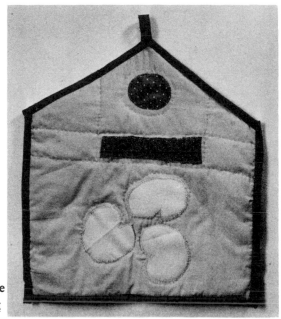

Plate
74

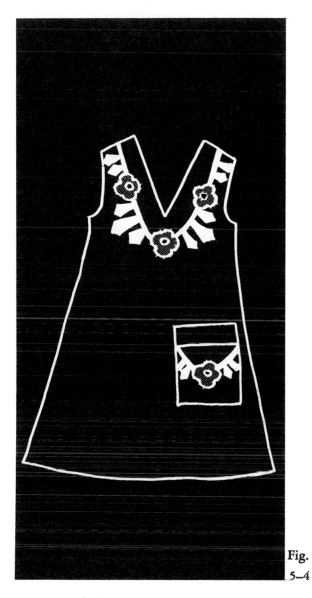

Fig.
5—4

2. A design may also be zig-zag or satin stitched in place. Zig-zag is a good stitch for knit fabrics. Proceed as before by cutting out the applique shape and pinning it in place. Loosen the tension on the sewing machine. Stitch around the design once with a wide zig-zag stitch. Go around a second time with a narrower zig-zag stitch or satin stitch. The tea cosy was appliqued in this way (plates 73, 74).

3. A design may be appliqued on a block (piece of fabric) either by hand or on the sewing machine. The block can then in turn be appliqued on a handbag, a dress, a pocket, or a yoke of a shirt.

4. Applique designs may be padded or quilted. This works best with large, simple shapes. To quilt, applique the design in place. Underneath the applique and the cloth it's sewn on, pin cotton batting and batiste. Sew through all four layers with running stitches or sewing machine stitches. Trim the batting to the seam.

Trim the batiste close to the seam. Finish the edge of the batiste with pinking shears. If greater fullness is desired, the design may now be padded. To pad, make a small opening in the back and insert extra batting with a small crochet hook or other pointed instrument.

139

Fig.
5–5

APPLIQUED PILLOWS—POCKETS FULL OF CHRISTMAS

Jan Eisenman's pillows (plate 75) illustrate what an imaginative use of machine applique can do. The front of the pillows are simple shapes with pockets in them which may be stuffed with toys if the pillow is being given to a child as a present.

1. Materials: plain cotton fabric (about one yard), scraps of printed cotton, felt, ribbons, laces, hooks, eyes, and buttons. The pillow slip consists of four pieces of plain cotton fabric: the front, the back, a third piece almost as long as the back to form a large pocket, and a shorter piece to make the flap (it should be long enough to overlap the pocket).

2. On a piece of paper from twelve to fifteen inches square, make a drawing. You may copy the pillow shown or design your own, perhaps adapting an illustration from a children's book.

3. Use your sketch as a pattern to cut out the shapes for the applique. Fold the uncut scraps of fabric in half so that when you cut, you cut two of each shape. Of course, add a quarter of an inch all around for seams. Seam the double pieces together by machine, wrong side out and turn them. Be sure to clip the curves. This is easier than trying to turn the edges of the small pieces under and hem them by hand.

4. When you have completed the separate appliques, pin or baste them onto the pillow face, overlapping the larger pieces. Stitch them down by machine close to the edge, leaving openings to form pockets. Start with the center pieces and work outward. Sew on buttons, hooks and eyes, snaps and other trimmings.

5. To assemble the pillowcase, first hem the free edge at the top of the pocket piece and the free edge of the flap. Then lay the pillow front on the table with the appliqued side up. On top of this place the flap, right side down; then the pocket piece, right side down; then the back, right side down. Stitch together along top and sides leaving an opening along the bottom side to insert the stuffing. Turn the pillow right side out. Stuff. Fold the edges of the opening of the pillow in and close with tiny stitches.

141

Plate
75

142

TRAPUNTO

Trapunto or Italian quilting is often used as a form of decoration for collars, cuffs, handbags, and pillows. It is a way of padding a quilted design without using a filling layer. The steps are similar to the ones described in the quilting chapter.

1. For the surface, choose any tightly woven fabric: cotton, linen, silk, or satin. For the backing choose a loosely woven fabric: muslin, batiste, or cheesecloth.

2. The backing is basted to the face. A simple outline drawing is made on the backing in pencil. Flowers, scrolls, and geometric shapes are usual.

3. A line of running stitches is made on either side of the penciled line.

4. Bulky orlon yarn is threaded through the lines with a large yarn needle. At sharp angles or acute curves in the design, bring the needle out leaving a small loop. Reinsert the needle into the same channel and continue. The loops are made to allow for the possibility of shrinkage.

QUILTING SMALL OBJECTS

Small objects are more easily quilted than large ones because they can be more easily manipulated. The methods for quilting small objects are slightly different from those used for quilting bedcovers.

1. The easiest and simplest method for quilting small objects is to use straight pins to hold the layers together while quilting. Lay the patchwork or appliqued piece of cloth on muslin or other soft material. Cut around the shape. Remove the top layer. Spread batting on the backing and trim roughly. Put the top layer on the bottom two layers. Sometimes it helps to steam iron the three layers together. Starting in the center pin outward in a rough spiral (fig. 5-6). The article is now ready to be quilted.

2. The choice of hand versus machine quilting must now be made. On a small article, one can take the luxury of hand sewing. It does not take much time, and the hand sewn line has a special quality. The tea cosy seen in plates 73, 74 was

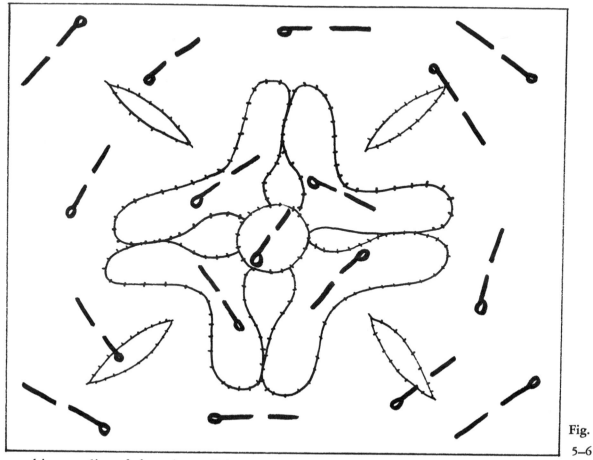

Fig. 5–6

machine appliqued, but the quilting was done by hand because I felt hand sewn quilting lines would frame and bring out the design. On the other hand, if an all-over design is used and the stitching is not part of the design, then the speed of machine sewing makes more sense. The "stripey" glasses case (plate 63) and the "Cotton Reel" handbag (plate 64) were quilted on the sewing machine. No matter which method you choose, remember to quilt out from the center. This is the best method of easing the puckers.

Another method of quilting small objects calls for the use of the quilting frame. Small quilting frames have tradi-tionally put in their appearance for quilting crib quilts and petticoats. The long bars should be one inch by two inches by three to four feet. The side bars should be one inch by two inches by two to three feet. The frame is clamped together at the corners with "C" clamps. Muslin backing is stretched across the frame and is firmly stitched to the cloth covering the long bars. The batting is spread across the backing. The top layer is laid on top of the bottom two layers. It is then basted in place. The batting is trimmed to the edge of the top layer. Quilt according to the instructions given in the Quilting chapter. (fig. 5-7)

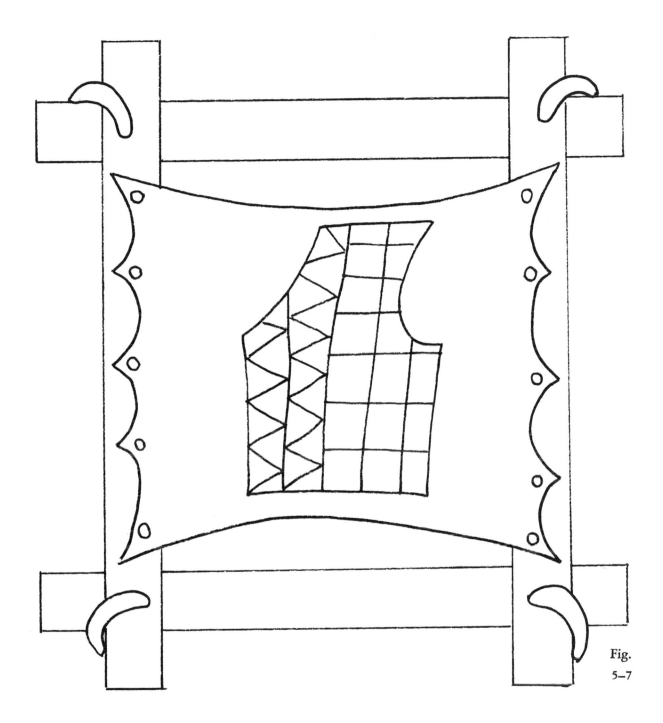

Fig. 5–7

NEW QUILTS, NEW FORMS

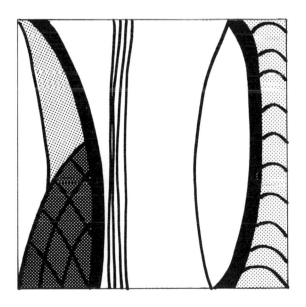

In recent years we have seen a revival and metamorphosis of handcrafts. Their function has altered from that of a utilitarian albeit ornamented object to an object that is made for the sheer sake of its handmade beauty. Artists and designers who in the past worked solely with paper, paint, canvas, metal, etc. have been turning to soft materials and have been making hangings, banners, soft sculptures, and wall "quilts." This chapter explores some of these new quilts and new forms and gives the artist's comments on their personal methodology of construction and design. Their designs may suggest ideas which you may choose to introduce into your own quiltmaking, or you may see the possibility of evolving your own forms from traditional quilts.

As a child, Helen Bitar made traditional samplers. In art school in Washington, Helen majored in printmaking and took the only course in fabric design they offered. There she began doing stitchery which she liked because it was portable and could even be worked on in a bar where a group of students gathered after classes.

It always rained in Seattle, and therefore color came to play an especially important role in her work because it was a way of making her own sun in an otherwise drab locality. Helen taught herself a few stitches from books and then began experimenting. Her designs were partially influenced by South American Indian patterns, but they have truly become her own personal vision. Most of her stitchery shapes are made with the satin stitch (fig. 6-1) and relatively thick materials (ribbons, many different types of yarn, metallic threads, etc.) so the lines of color are a single row of stitches deep.

Her basic design motifs are shown here used in two very different quilts. One consists of forty-two blocks. Each block is a different embroidered emblem (color plate 14). The other quilt combines an intricate piecing of small, many-colored silk rectangles with the embroidered emblems (color plate 1). The quilt builds outward from a central embroidered shape with this intricate piecing until it reaches the first set of framing borders which are interrupted by more embroidered medallions. The central area becomes a more clearly defined, purple,

cross-like shape which is framed with a yellow border. More small rectangles form a multi-colored border completing the quilt. The rectangles were pieced on the sewing machine. When Helen had finished this top, she went to the near-by Morman church in Missoula, Montana where the local ladies helped her quilt it. The women put the quilt into a traditional frame, and she and the women worked on it afternoons accompanied by lemonade and cookies until the quilting was finished. The women quilted to help raise money for the church. This is still a common practice in many parts of America.

Sophia Adler from Westbury, New York makes very large applique hangings. She writes of herself and her work: "As you may have sensed from my work, I have long admired traditional patchquilts. Perhaps some of that feeling has sifted into my wall hangings. Though much of my work includes stitchery-embroidery overlaid onto applique, the 'Flowers of Dusk' (4 by 8 feet) (color plate 3) is done with only solid-colored cottons and silks sewn together with running and blind stitches onto a fabric backing by hand." No quilting frame was used.

Ms. Adler goes on to describe her method of design: "I start out by suspending a fabric backing from a rod on the wall, then pin and sew directly onto that backing. At the most, I might have a rough preliminary sketch of the effect I hope to get. The design comes about by placing pieces of fabric and appliqued work next to each other on the backing and then seeing what might happen."

Amy Stromsten of New York City used

Plate
76

149

the traditional "Maple Leaf" pattern for her contemporary photographic wall quilt (color plate 24). The leaves are cut out from photographs printed on photo-sensitized linen. The surface of the linen is, "specially prepared to be exposed under an enlarger and is processed in exactly the same manner as a normal print on paper. After the linen is dried, I can cut and sew it. The image is permanent and will not wash off." She uses the traditional quilt form to comment on social conditions. Each of the maple leaves is pieced from a different photograph. She writes of the photographs, "(they) are meant to be an ironic comment on America. Rather than showing quaint landscapes, I choose photographs of the abuse of the American countryside. There is a photo of a subdivision with very poor site planning; there are photos of signs placed in beautiful places; scenes of American problems, such as the unemployment line in New York. These photographs are contrasted with simple landscapes . . . and textures of water and clouds." Her final intention, however, is decorative, and "the bright colors as well as the leaf pattern give (the quilt) unity." "The quilting was not done on a frame, but rather each square was stuffed with cotton batting and then attached to the others. All sewing was done on the sewing machine, except the final piecing together of the blocks, which was done by hand."

Jodi Robbin is a Californian artist who uses batik, a way of making images with wax resist and fabric dye. She explains, "Emir's Palace (plate 76, color plate 22) is a partly-quilted wall hanging composed of two pieces of batiste cotton batiks with silk and mirror insets." One of her other quilts made with Sally Woodbridge (plate 77) consists of a batik zebra, the word zebra, and the mirror image of the word all appliqued onto a piece of white pre-quilted material. Of her methods she says, "I've never used a quilting frame but do use some machine zig-zag . . . I love to do hand stitchery."

Michiko Sato is a designer and artist in Yonkers, New York who has made appliqued and embroidered wall hangings. She appliqued one block of "The Hudson River Quilt." Recently she has turned to making patchwork bed and wall quilts on the sewing machine. She tells the following story of the evolution of her designs. "I began making patchwork bedspreads because I had a lot of scraps from sewing clothes for my three girls. My first interest was to use every bit of the scrap . . . , create designs so the cutting would be simple (using cuts along the grain or tearing), and to be able to do the sewing on the machine. By limiting the cutting and sewing process, I was able to realize an idea (depending on the size . . . single to king size) in anywhere from thirty-five to seventy hours. First I worked with strips of material. Court House Squares and Log Cabin designs used strips perfectly." She began experimenting with her own designs and made two quilts. "I became intrigued in texture . . . the surprising effects of combining prints and colors. I became aware of the importance of value (the lightness and the darkness) and tried 'Pink Crosses' (color plate 20). The effect was all right but my cutting and sewing left much to be desired. I began to really appreciate the craftsmanship of the old quilts. Then, I saw the Whitney

Plate
77

151

Museum show. The variety, texture, and size impressed and inspired me to concentrate on more patchwork experiments." There were three more quilts made in which she experimented with cross and diamond shapes. Next the "Brown and Black Pinwheel Quilt" was made (color plate 21). The pinwheel pattern was made by piecing eight half square triangles into four squares and then sewing the four squares together to form a block. Where the diagonals converge (either at the center of the block or where four blocks meet), the sewing machine must go through eight layers of cloth. Ms. Sato says of the process of making pinwheel quilts, "(the quilt) was started from the center and worked outward. It was hard on my sewing machine sewing the corners with eight layers of cloth. When I made another one with pinwheels, my machine crunched up and jammed . . . it has never recovered from the strain so the diagonals are out." "Kimono Quilt" (color plate 23) was made next. Ms. Sato states: "Right now, I'm making diamonds of two-inch squares (to use scraps of scraps) to see if I could get the effect of 'Grandmother's Flower Garden' that uses hexagons." She concludes, "I have made nine pieces since the Whitney show and I still feel intrigued with the medium."

Ann Wooster of New York City sees quilting as a structural extension of her sculpture. "Quilting has always seemed to me like a mechanical device, a way of providing structure and joining things together. The first quilted object I made other than pot holders was a set of seven foot pea pods. The quilting gave shape to the sides of the pods. My most recent 'quilts' have been of clear plastic so that

Plate 78 "Stolen Cars"; 1972; metal toy cars and vinyl; 41" × 60"; made by the author

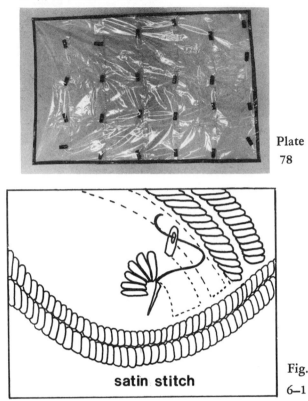

Plate 78

satin stitch

Fig. 6–1

the middle, hidden layer may be seen. A clear plastic quilt also seems to have the mystery and frustration of blister packaging. One quilt is called 'Stolen Cars' (plate 78). I made it by first buying three packages of toy metal cars then painting them Chinese red. The cars were heat sealed onto plastic using an iron and a ruler to make the lines. The edge is bound in red tape. If I had used a lighter weight plastic I could have quilted it together on the sewing machine. I called the quilt "Stolen Cars" because the process of painting them reminded me of stories I had read of secret workshops where stolen cars were repainted and given new license plates. The green car in the lower right

152

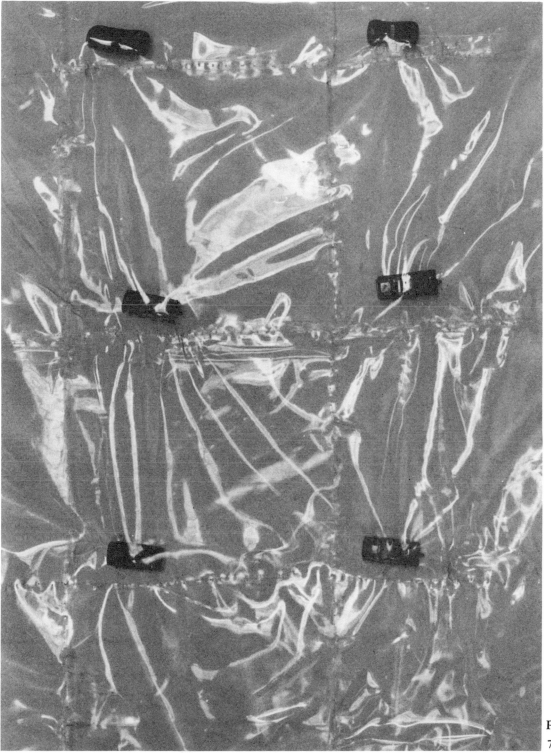

Plate
79

Plate 79 Detail of "Stolen Cars"

hand corner of the quilt was a bow to the traditional quilting superstition from the 1800's that only God can create a perfect thing, and that if a human produced an object without flaw, it would call the Devil and misfortune would follow. In the nineteenth century, they made green flowers and blue leaves; I broke the uniformity of having only red cars by sealing a green car into one plastic pocket."

Bonnie Gisel lives in Rochester, New York. She is a former painter who has turned to using soft materials, and the way she talks about her materials reflects her fine arts background. For the last few years she has also been collecting old quilts from auctions, flea markets, and thrift shops in the Rochester area, and she now has a large collection of quilts which she finds an influence on her art. ". . . Because I have little contact with other people who are working, I am relating more to the quilt collection. . . . I never thought of my constructions as being quilt-like, but since I have begun my own quilt collection I can relate to the ladies who created these incredible pieces of American Fine-Folk art better than to any artist or art movement. I do not own one quilt that denotes poor craftsmanship or poor design. . . ."

She explains why she stopped painting: "I began working with cloth constructions because paint became mechanical, unreal, and impersonal for me. It wasn't me." She continues on as to why she prefers working with quilting material: "I incorporated the use of dye to color the canvas and other materials I use because it was a color which penetrated the fabric. It did not lie on the surface but became part of the thing I was making. . . . The

Plate 80 "Box Pod Quilt"; 1971; muslin, canvas, and mattress padding; stitched and dyed; made by Bonnie Gisel

Plate 80

constructions were a different kind of control. It wasn't just stretching a canvas and painting it because it was the only way it could go. I could let something grow. I could learn a different kind of control. I could take a hard form, a square cut from canvas, stitch a line on it (a drawing), and dye it. It was not as hard

Plate 81 Detail of "Box Pod Quilt"

Plate
81

meanings or feelings. By using a tight machine stitch, a very hard form is created; by using a very open hand stitch, a sort of dotted, loose, less mechanical feeling is created. I incorporate many different stitches in my constructions."

Three of Bonnie's quilt constructions are shown here. The "Pink and Blue Quilt," 1971 (color plate 16) was made by taking a large sheet of canvas and cutting twenty-five holes into it. Each space was filled with a stitched "drawing" (her term for cloth with sewn lines on it) on folded, pleated, dyed canvas. Some of these "drawings" are machine stitched in place and some are hand stitched into place.

The "Box Pod Quilt," 1971 (plate 80) was made from rough texture canvas, muslin, and mattress padding which is stitched and dyed. A three layer circular form (two donuts enclosing a third piece of fabric) (see detail in plate 81) was machine and handstitched in place. She uses the "quilt-like, repetitive forms, utilizing variations in circular units to create a flow in the piece."

The "Remade Block Blanket," 1972 (plate 82, color plate 12) is an extremely repetitive quilt construction. Each unit has its own characteristic 3½ by 4 inch rectangle each of which is dyed separately, then machine stitched together with a small stitch creating a very tight line. About half of the rectangular inserts are stitched by hand causing the squares to "breath a little more." Canvas was used for rectangular windows, but the inserts are made of rayon, wool, blanketing, and gathered material.

Bonnie Gisel sometimes pokes holes in the surface of the quilt top, but Nell

as before; it had become soft and obtainable."

"I work with repetitive forms, creating units or modules which are then put together (usually on the sewing machine) to make a larger square, rectangle, or box-like form. I like the idea of being able to control these units. I can use the same unit, alter it, give it its own characteristics such as a different line (machine stitched), and create constructions all the same yet each different, utilizing only very subtle changes in color and design. Manipulating is a good word to describe what I do when I create a construction, altering the boxes or units until each is in its right space when they are stitched together."

She uses, "a sewing machine to create lines." "By changing the stitch and also by hand stitching, different lines can be created which in turn have different

Plate 82 "Remade Block Blanket"; 1972; 8' × 6'; canvas, wool, rayon, and cotton; dyed and stitched; made by Bonnie Gisel

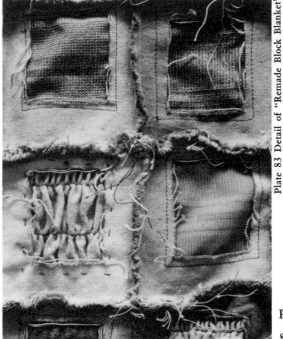

Plate 83 Detail of "Remade Block Blanket"

Plate 82

Plate 83

Booker Sonneman of Chevy Chase, Maryland carries the destruction of the flatbed surface of the quilt top to its logical conclusion. She constructs sculptures out of quilted ribbons and areas of fabric which have, in most cases, become totally three dimensional and do not relate at all to the flat top. The quilted ribbons and areas are combined with applique, threads, and yarns. Details of the head of "The Being at the Forest Entrance" (color plate 9) and the head and skirt of "The Woman Clothed by the Sun" (color plate 6) give a clear feeling of how the materials are manipulated for her purposes.

Nell Sonneman describes her methods of working, attitudes toward materials, and sources of inspiration and design: ". . . the materials I use are almost exclusively commercial yard goods of every type, organic and synthetic, and the tech-nique is that used in quilts, applique with primary interest in the architectonic structure formed by the 'patches' and almost no interest in stitchery for its own sake."

When designing a new work, Nell Sonneman states that she is concerned with: "(1) what I need to say and (2) the nature of the materials I am using and how they behave naturally." "The two must get into conjunction. Colors, shapes of fabric pieces, darks and lights, and textures are all chosen initially as conforming most closely to what there is within me which must be expressed. The work shapes up when these all go together. How it is to come out is absolutely unpredictable. In this sense, it is closer to paint and sculpture than to the traditional quilter's use of pre-determined or calculated patterns."

"When I worked in closed space and

156

structured in terms of a flat, unbroken rectangle, I used hand work, mostly hem stitching. A dramatic change began to occur when I started using the zig-zag stitch of the sewing machine. A soft quality was lost in the change, but the gain was immeasurable."

"The machine enabled me to make sturdier constructions so that the rectangle could be penetrated by holes and could dissolve into fragmentations when it was suitable to the message. Still it is applique, without any question, although it looks very different. It is simply moving into open space. This change from closed to open was enormously freeing and exciting. And the dirty, old, villainous machine did it."

"To manage large sizes on the machine, the total design must be broken down into workable parts, much as a sculptor preparing for bronze casting must break up the statue after its modeling is complete. This requires considerable ingenuity so that these breaks will be an organic part of the design."

In "The Moonshot and the Transistor" (plate 84), Nell Sonneman suspends quilted and appliqued fabrics between two poles with large open spaces separating the pieces and making the wall function as a color. The moon is centered, and through a skillful juxtaposition of black and white and tan and black fabrics, she combines a feeling of deep space and the black and white photographic experience most of us had when viewing the actual moonshot.

Plate 84

Plate 85

Plate 84 "Moonshot and the Transistor"; 1969; 6⅓' × 5½'; applique and assorted fabrics; made by Nell Booker Sonneman; photograph by Charlie Brown

Plate 85 "Being at the Forest Entrance"; 1970; 6'2" × 1'10"; applique and assorted fabrics; made by Nell Booker Sonneman; photograph by Charlie Brown

Plate 86 "Woman Clothed with the Sun"; front view with the following part of the text showing: "Woman clothed with the sun and a moon under her feet and twelve stars upon her head"; 1971–72; 6' high; applique and assorted fabrics; made by Nell Booker Sonneman; photograph by Charlie Brown

"The Being at the Forest Entrance" (plate 85, color plate 7) and "The Woman Clothed by the Sun" (plate 86, color plate 5) both represent her most involved and evolved types of sculptures. The figures are made up of strips and areas of fabric suspended from a central crown or head. They are both six feet or over in height. One receives the impression of confronting oddly regal people when standing in front of them. The use of materials is very tactile, and the works almost demand to be touched.

Plate 87 "My name is Ishmael"; 1967; 48" × 3⅔'; applique and assorted fabrics; made by Nell Booker Sonneman; photographed by Charlie Brown

Plate
86

Plate
87

Bibliography

Butler, Anne. *Embroidery Stitches.* New York: Frederick A. Praeger, 1970.

Carlisle, Lilian Baker. *Pieced Work and Applique Quilts at the Shelburne Museum.* Shelburne: Shelburne Museum, 1957.

Colby, Avril. *Patchwork.* Boston: Charles T. Branford Company, 1958.

Colby, Avril. *Patchwork Quilts.* New York: Charles Scribner's Sons, 1965.

Dunton, William Rush. *Old Quilts.* Catonsville: William Rush Dunton, 1946.

Finley, Ruth E. *Old Patchwork Quilts and the Women Who Made Them.* Philadelphia: J. B. Lippincott Company, 1929.

Fitzrandolph, Mavis. *Traditional Quilting.* London: Batsford, 1954.

Hinson, Dolores A. *Quilting Manual.* New York: Hearthside Press, 1970.

Ickis, Marguerite. *The Standard Book of Quilt Making and Collecting.* New York: Dover Press, 1949.

Koke, Richard. "American Quilts: An Exhibition." *New York Historical Society Quarterly Annual Report.* Vol. XXXII, January-October, 1948.

Laliberté, Norman, and McIlhany, Sterling. *Banners and Hangings Design and Construction.* New York: Van Nostrand Reinhold Company, 1966.

159

Lane, Rose Wilder. *Woman's Day Book of American Needlework.* New York: Simon and Schuster, 1963.

Laury, Jean Ray. *Quilts and Coverlets, a Contemporary Approach.* New York: Van Nostrand Reinhold Company, 1970.

McCall's Needlework and Crafts magazine, Editors of. *McCall's Needlework Treasury.* New York: Random House, 1964.

McKim, Ruby Short. *One Hundred and One Patchwork Patterns.* New York: Dover Publications, 1962.

Peto, Florence. *American Quilts and Coverlets.* New York: Studio Publications, 1948.

Schuette, Marie. *A Pictorial History of Embroidery.* New York: Frederick A. Praeger, 1964.

Webster, Marie D. *Quilts, Their Story and How to Make Them.* Garden City: Doubleday, Doran and Company, 1928.

Index of Patchwork and Applique Quilt Names

General Index